PRAISE FOR *Bodega Stories*

"*Bodega Stories* kisses us awake! Amaris Castillo has written a gorgeous portrait of Dominican bodegas, vignettes fueled with love for her hard-working parents and her community. Much like the robust inventory of neighborhood bodegas, Castillo's book serves up a chorus of characters that fill in essential gaps to our American story. A joy to read!"

ANGIE CRUZ / author of *How Not to Drown in a Glass of Water*

"Everyone is familiar with the neighborhood bodega, but not everyone gets to know the inner workings of such places. *Bodega Stories* takes you behind the scenes, into the heart of one family's business. Its draw is magnetic and only strengthened by the tenderness and charm Castillo infuses into so many of her vignettes."

ANNABELLE TOMETICH / author of *The Mango Tree: A Memoir of Fruit, Florida, and Felony*

"*Bodega Stories* gives voice to the working-class immigrants from the Caribbean who often play such important roles in community building, those who create safe spaces for gathering like bodegas, barbershops, salones de belleza, and mom-and-pop restaurants. Castillo's descriptions are rich and layered, giving a sense of place and situating the reader beautifully inside each nook and cranny of Orlando Latin Market."

ERIKA MORILLO / author of *Mother Archive: A Dominican Family Memoir*

"I love this book. *Bodega Stories* is a joyful portrait not only of Castillo's family and their bodega but also of the larger community of immigrants hailing from the Caribbean and Latin America that come to Orlando Latin Market in search of home. Castillo gracefully weaves together the memories, interviews, and stories of her family and customers with loving detail and the precision of a poet."

CLAIRE JIMÉNEZ / author of *What Happened to Ruthy Ramirez*

"With care, insight and sensitivity, Castillo captures what makes bodegas so important and necessary. In depicting her parents' experience operating Orlando Latin Market, Castillo introduces us to the community upon which the bodega depends—bringing to life a vibrant multicultural, multilingual, multigenerational community, shining a light on people who are often overlooked, and holding space for those who are often crowded out."

AMINA GAUTIER / author of *The Best That You Can Do*

BODEGA STORIES

UNIVERSITY PRESS OF FLORIDA Florida A&M University, Tallahassee
Florida Atlantic University, Boca Raton / Florida Gulf Coast University, Ft. Myers
Florida International University, Miami / Florida State University, Tallahassee / New College of Florida, Sarasota / University of Central Florida, Orlando / University of Florida, Gainesville
University of North Florida, Jacksonville / University of South Florida, Tampa / University of West Florida, Pensacola

Bodega Stories
Amaris Castillo

3515
HORARIO
LUNES @ SABADO
8 AM-7PM
DOMINGO
9 AM
@
4 PM
NOTICE
ADT
MALTA INDIA
PEPES

Amaris Castillo

BODEGA STORIES

UNIVERSITY PRESS OF FLORIDA Gainesville / Tallahassee
Tampa / Boca Raton / Pensacola / Orlando / Miami / Jacksonville / Ft. Myers / Sarasota

Cover: Designed by Mindy Basinger Hill. Illustration created using images provided courtesy of the author and images from Adobe Stock.

31 30 29 28 27 26 6 5 4 3 2 1

LIBRARY OF CONGRESS CATALOGING-IN-PUBLICATION DATA

Names: Castillo, Amaris author
Title: Bodega stories / Amaris Castillo.
Description: Gainesville : University Press of Florida, 2026.
Identifiers: LCCN 2026010847 (print) | LCCN 2026010848 (ebook) | ISBN 9780813081595 paperback | ISBN 9780813075464 ebook
Subjects: LCSH: Orlando Latin Market (St. Petersburg, Fla.) | Grocers—Florida—Saint Petersburg | Hispanic American consumers—Florida—Saint Petersburg | Grocery shopping—Florida—Saint Petersburg | Grocery trade—Florida—Saint Petersburg | Cooking, Latin American | LCGFT: Anecdotes
Classification: LCC HD9321.9.O756 C37 2026 (print) | LCC HD9321.9.O756 (ebook)
LC record available at https://lccn.loc.gov/2026010847
LC ebook record available at https://lccn.loc.gov/2026010848

The University Press of Florida is the scholarly publishing agency for the State University System of Florida, comprising Florida A&M University, Florida Atlantic University, Florida Gulf Coast University, Florida International University, Florida State University, New College of Florida, University of Central Florida, University of Florida, University of North Florida, University of South Florida, and University of West Florida.

University Press of Florida
PO Box 140239
Gainesville, FL 32614
floridapress.org

GPSR EU Authorized Representative: Mare Nostrum Group B.V, Doelen 72, 4831 GR Breda, The Netherlands, gpsr@mare-nostrum.co.uk

Este libro está dedicado a mis padres, Damaris y Freddy.

GRACIAS POR TODO.

For Mami and Papi.

THANK YOU FOR EVERYTHING.

CONTENTS

LA COCINA

WE OUTSIDE

LA OFICINA (STORAGE ROOM)

BODEGA STORIES

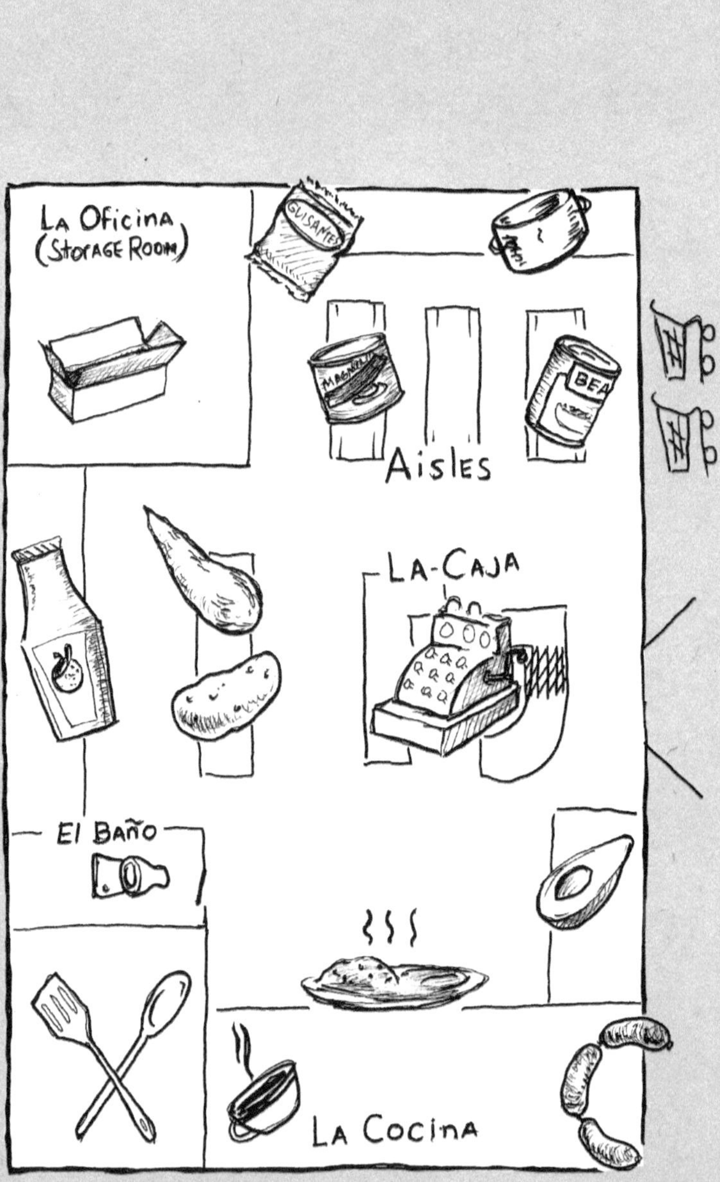

BODEGA FLOOR PLAN

ORLANDO LATIN MARKET

Drive through St. Petersburg, down US 19. Make a right on Thirtieth Avenue North, pass Hartford Street North, and you'll see it between a coin laundromat and a barbershop. A bodega the length of a gas station, with a dozen or so parking spots. This isn't the typical bodega you'd find in New York City. After all, we're in Florida. But it's a bodega nonetheless, owned for more than two decades by married couple Freddy and Damaris Castillo. My parents.

A large rectangular sign, flat and yellow, looms over all who enter the business. It reads ORLANDO LATIN MARKET in dark blue lettering. An illustration of a ham hock, a garlic bulb, and an onion sits between the words LATIN and MARKET. Below the store's name is a two-word invitation: BODEGA LATINA.

And like bodegas back in Brooklyn, the sign lists the store's offerings:

Latin foods to go
Deli-meats & groceries
Original Cuban sandwiches
Breakfast & lunch

A banner made of flags under Orlando Latin Market's building-length awning indicates the products you'll find inside hail from multiple countries. The pieces of cloth flap in the wind above the heads of customers. El Salvador, Colombia, Cuba, Panama, Costa Rica, Puerto Rico, Venezuela, Honduras, the United States. There is also the flag of the Dominican Republic, a country that shares the island of Hispaniola with Haiti. Both my parents are from DR. The Caribbean nation's flag—with its white cross on a background of alternating blue and red rectangles—hangs between Bolivia and Ecuador. The flags don't all move in the same direction. Where one whips furiously, another one sways gently. The elements have frayed most of their edges. Just beyond the flags are perched wooden parrots. The first is the color of the ocean, the second mostly teal with pink, yellow, and green feather tails, and the third a mix of coral, bright green, and blue. The fourth parrot is missing. All will later be replaced by shinier, brighter parrots.

The bodega's storefront is wide, with big windows framed by red brick. Outside is a garbage bin and two newsstands carrying copies of *Auto Connection* and *Inmigración.* There's an ATM in a metal encasing painted red, with a soft plastic flap you lift to access your money. Atop the computerized machine are clay vases, a nice decorative touch courtesy of Damaris, my mother, and her love of greenery. At home, she fills her screened terraza with plants and orchids. And here, to the left of the ATM, are even taller plants in clay pots. Alive and thriving. To the right of the entrance door are mismatched shopping carts for customers with long grocery lists. A big metal merchandiser containing bags of ice doubles as a high-top table. This is where a small group of cubanos hang out most mornings. The Cuban men lean against the slanted freezer unit, sip their espresso, and talk. And talk. And talk.

In 2002, my family said goodbye to New York and moved to Florida. Papi had left months before we did, to scout the Tampa Bay area in search of a new place for us to live. Having been to Florida before (see: the many theme parks in Orlando), I was enamored by its promise of sun and fun. New York City, my home, was all I knew. I was born and raised in the Crown Heights neighborhood of Brooklyn. We lived there for the first decade of my life before we moved to Queens, where my parents bought a house in Woodhaven. When you grow up somewhere, you become deeply familiar with its rhythms. I could easily trace the contours of my world there, my senses by then attuned to Nueba Yol's smells, sounds, and sights. I knew of its vastness, of its bitter cold, of its sidewalks with blackened spots of chewing gum, of its warmth and attitude and stench. I knew as much as I could know at that stage of my adolescence.

But Florida, from which we would carve out our new life, was an exciting unknown. At first, I felt giddy about moving there. It was a shiny new state that was, for the most part, largely unexplored by my family. And I was especially happy for Papi, who would no longer have to deal with the winters he so despised. In fact, once a Florida resident, my father would joke and say, *No quiero ir pa' Nueba Yol ni en foto.* He was adamant about that. He never wanted to return to New York, not even in a photo. If you were planning to visit NYC and had so much as a palm-sized photo of Freddy Castillo in your wallet, you best be pulling the picture from its plastic insert. Just leave my father and his face behind. Whenever Pa said this, I'd laugh. I'd think he was being extra, un exagerao. But there was always an undercurrent of seriousness in his voice.

Turns out my father went through a lot as a bodeguero in Nueba Yol. Our New Yorks were very different. A longtime bodega worker, Freddy did not experience the same city that I experienced. I wouldn't learn about his city, or what he endured, until I was much older.

As a Florida resident, Pa would be able to drop his shoulders some. He looked forward to doing what he loved: fishing in calm waters. And maybe Mami would be happier now, with her husband and children under the same roof again.

It is one thing to visit Florida, and it's another to grind out a daily life in this state. First of all, it's hot as shit down here. In the summer months, the sun will beat your skin tender and grill you like a carne asada. We face hurricanes, environmental hazards, rising property taxes, certain politicians. But I was about fourteen years old when we moved, and I wouldn't have known about all this baggage. My family settled in a Clearwater house built in the 1970s with dated cabinets and a floor-length mirrored wall in the living room. I remember walking through our new home and taking in my bright, airy room. Excited for what was next.

Much like any relationship, my honeymoon phase with Florida quickly dissipated as I struggled to find my place in a high school where almost everyone grew up together. When my mom asked me if I wanted a quinceañera, I scoffed. *Who would attend? Who would we even invite?* We were now living in an area without any close relatives nearby with the exception of one of my mom's older sisters, Tía Margarita, who moved in with us after her divorce. Later, my Titi Rosi and her family also left New York for Tampa. And there was my Tía Yolanda, who owned a house in Tampa with her family but didn't live there year-round. On weekdays after school, I'd rush home to watch *Rebelde*, a Mexican telenovela about teenagers at a private school who form a band. I lived vicariously through these characters in hourly increments, wishing real life was as exhilarating. I made friends quickly but often felt afloat. Some of this may very well have been teen angst, but I was eager to graduate and jump-start my life, whatever that meant to my teenage mind.

Fast-forward to 2005, my freshman year at the University of South Florida, where I stayed in a dorm on the main Tampa campus. By then I had fully adjusted to Florida life, though I never forgot about New York. Sometime that year, my parents informed me that they wanted to buy a bodega. I was thrilled for them because they had been trudging along in various jobs, Mami at Walmart, Papi in construction, and their work wasn't going as well as we'd hoped. One time, my father came home with a box of oranges instead of the money he was owed for his labor. They both deserved so much more. Growing up in Brooklyn, I watched my parents own or work in different bodegas, so they knew the business intimately.

The bodega life is grueling. The hours are long and the days bleed into weeks and through holidays. It can be isolating. There are also many physical demands to the job. In New York and other major cities, bodega workers must lift, carry, and move heavy boxes, retrieve items from storage, and bring boxes down to the basement—if they have one. It is all-consuming, because sometimes one bodega worker will be tasked with being the cashier, the manager, and the person who stocks the shelves. But here Ma and Pa were, wanting to be their own bosses again. *We were looking for bodega bodega bodega bodega,* Ma recalls. *We'd go around asking in Clearwater, in St. Pete. We saw many bodegas, but none were a good fit.* Then one day, Papi's tío—a bodeguero himself—called up my dad. He'd heard from a vendor that there was a bodega for sale in St. Pete. It was called Orlando Latin Market. Pa wanted to see it for himself, so he drove there. Once inside, he noticed the store didn't have much merchandise. Some items had passed their expiration dates. The refrigeration wasn't where it could be. *They didn't sell candles,* Pa remembers. *They didn't sell beer.* Mami thought it needed work. But she and Papi agreed on one thing. This place had promise. My father tells me, *Your mamá and I felt there was a future here.* They thought about it, discussed it at length. Then they made an offer. It was accepted. SOLD.

As the new owners of Orlando Latin Market, they got to work. *In the beginning it was not easy,* Ma says. They changed a great deal, brought in new fridges, worked with vendors to bring in more and more merchandise. *No fue fácil. It was difficult, but with time we grew the business.* For continuity, they kept the name of the store as is.

Step inside today and you'll walk into an explosion of color and products, from Cuban crackers and sweet medianoche bread to shelves with over-the-counter medicines, Vapuru (see: VapoRub), Dominican leave-in conditioners, topical analgesics for aches and dolores, and the Agua de Violetas spray so loved by Cuban mothers. There are liquid dietary supplements like Rabano Yodado from El Salvador and even balsamo ruso—a Russian balm used by some customers for its healing properties. To your left, parallel to the store's front wall, is an open-air cooler filled with plátanos, green peppers, limes, bunches of cilantro and culantro, and other produce. There's a carnicería, a small meat counter—its deli case lined with cuts of beef, chicken, and pork. And next to it is the front kitchen, where there are usually two or three Cuban women (and sometimes Mami or my Tía Margarita) in hairnets and gloves, serving food, frituras (fritters), and steaming cups of café con leche to customers.

My relationship with the business in its infancy was complicated. I appreciated Orlando Latin Market because I saw what its earnings did for our family. The bodega kept the mortgage paid. It was the reason Ma or Pa would often have cash to give me when I needed it, and why they could help me with emergency expenses. Managing the bodega day-to-day was a heavy load but, at the end of the day, my parents were their own bosses. La jefa y el jefe. There is a certain level of autonomy in that.

But this was also a place where I often felt claustrophobic behind the register counter, faced with the need to defend myself and my parents' honor at any given moment. And where, in my early twenties, I was subjected to the creepy male gaze. In young adulthood, the cashier position became my placeholder job until I figured out my next move. My parents would wake me up early in the morning and off we'd head to the bodega. But once we arrived, I'd often make a beeline to the storage room in the back corner of the bodega. There, surrounded by pallets of canned goods and boxes stacked high, Mami had a small cot for me with a pillow. I'd sleep for an hour or so before I had to wake up to work.

Damaris and Freddy had only me and my brother—also Freddy—in that order. Which makes me the older one. There are whole studies about the experiences of the eldest child of immigrants, as there should be. As the eldest, you are a cultural broker. You have most likely served as interpreter out in public. You have ordered for family members at restaurants. You have read dry letters from government agencies in English and tried to make sense of them in Spanish. It means you were the first child to be educated in the US from pre-K—also a first for your parents. For me, it especially meant that I tried to be a dutiful daughter. I was there for my parents when they needed me at the bodega. How could I not be? Helping with the family business was the right thing to do.

My parents were building up Orlando Latin Market at the same time that I was adjusting to college. It was a solid forty minutes or so from the bodega to USF. I didn't have a car, so my dad would sometimes pick me up on Fridays so I could help them all weekend. If he was busy, one of his employees, Molina, would drive the store van and pick me up at my dorm. On those drives back to Pinellas County, I'd watch my university shrink in the side-view mirror. I'd think about the fun I could be having on Saturday night and all of Sunday, but instead I'd be spending my weekend stuck in a bodega for hours on my feet. There were times when my mom would call me to see if I could help them at the store over the weekend. A few times, I lied and said I had to study for an exam the following week. Because my education was always considered paramount, she'd immediately back off. I still feel a tinge of guilt when I think about that.

But those moments were few and far between. I have always felt

FREDDY AND HIS DAUGHTER, AMARIS, FROM
BEHIND THE REGISTER AT ORLANDO LATIN MARKET.

indebted to my parents in a way I can't fully articulate (and should probably be working out in therapy). When I thought about all my parents had done for me and my brother, my mind would adjust accordingly. I could never repay them for all their sacrifices, and I don't believe they expect me to. My mom and dad may not even think as deeply about all this as I do because they work all the time. But at the very least, I could try to repay them by excelling in school, graduating from college, and by helping as a cajera in their store. I'm not alone in feeling this knot of guilt and responsibility to make one's parents proud. Many other children of immigrants identify with this same debt, this same guilt. So I stepped up. What I needed to do and what I wanted to do were one and the same. I worked alongside my parents, even filling in for them whenever they had to go on pressing errands or travel to the Dominican Republic.

Once my parents had grown the business and settled into a groove, there came a time when Papi became restless. He wanted to step away from it all. Mami says they had had the bodega for three, maybe four years when he approached her. He was tired from the bodega grind. *And I understood him,* she says, *because he'd been working in bodegas since he was eighteen years old.* The thought of selling the bodega was floated. But Ma didn't want to. *I said, "No, no, no. We can't sell the store because we are still young. And I don't want to go back to working elsewhere."* She suggested they instead hand over the managerial duties to the carnicero at the time. The butcher could take over the store for two years, and Mami could continue working there. It would be a demotion of sorts for her, temporarily, but she didn't care.

Papi had high hopes for his new business venture. He wanted to sell palms—tall, picturesque plants that bring tropical charm to Florida homes. If and when his new business took off, Ma said she would consider staying home. She recalled telling him: "*But for now I will keep working, because we need the money.*" The bodega, she tells me, is what they knew. *I saw a future here. Even if we were tired and all that. Because here I saw a future—that we would be able to echar pa'lante.* They'd be able to push forward, to progress.

They decided to hand Orlando Latin Market over to the butcher who was hardworking and trustworthy. Time went on, and Papi's new business unfortunately didn't go well. He eventually returned to the bodega. And when he did, Mami noticed a change. She says my father came back with renewed vigor. *It's like he said, "This is what I know, and this is what I like." He came back with more ánimo. I saw how he came back. I saw the difference.*

With time and great sacrifice, Orlando Latin Market continued to thrive. Freddy and Damaris worked together and alongside their employees, many of whom were Cuban. After closing, Ma and Pa would drive home, eat dinner, shower, decompress, and sleep. Then they'd wake up the next day and do it all over again.

Ask me why I wrote *Bodega Stories* and you will find an origami of reasons. There are layers to it, many reasons folded into and over each other. All my life, I've recognized bodegas—these small owner-operated convenience stores—as community anchors. In New York City, many are open 24/7. They provide the essentials like milk, eggs, and bread. But many also carry products from the countries their owners hail from, including DR, Yemen, Mexico, and Bangladesh. As a child, I developed a keen understanding that the bodega was important to not only my family but to the people they served. This space gives me a sense of grounding and familiarity that I find comforting, no matter who owns it.

I wanted to present a written record of this place, of this dot on the St. Petersburg map, in this particular time of Florida's history. Curiosity about the lives of the employees and customers who filter in and out of Orlando Latin Market also fueled me. I wanted to understand what brought them here. This book is an exercise in memory, in language, in history. It is about people and about the stories we tell ourselves about who we are and where we come from. The personal accounts of everyday folks are worth our attention. We can understand who we are by examining who we were, and by revisiting the worlds that built us. The stories you'll find in this book are not exhaustive at all, but slices of stories people were willing to share with me.

As a young girl, I loved to observe my father interact with customers.

In the bodega, stories had life, and I was their captive audience. This was years before I decided to pursue journalism as a career, and long before I felt comfortable calling myself a storyteller. But there were many early signs. In first grade, I won a storytelling contest. I must have been around six years old. My mom kept a Xeroxed photo of me at the P.S. 316 auditorium, standing alongside the other winners. I don't remember the contest, but I absolutely believe I had a story to tell. My family is filled with effortless storytellers. They could just be talking, but what comes out are accounts that meander deliciously. Stories that you savor long after they're done. At family parties as a girl, I'd hang out with my cousins then sneak over to the kitchen, where Mami and her sisters, my tías, would often gather. There I'd be, listening in on their conversations that ascended in excitement and descended just as fast.

When we lived in Brooklyn, Mami regularly took us to the main branch of the Brooklyn Public Library, where we'd often borrow as many books as we could carry home. I devoured books, often begging my mom to let me read one more chapter before bed. I wanted to stay in these pages and other worlds a bit longer. I have a vivid memory from Robert H. Goddard Middle School 202 in Ozone Park, Queens, where I got hit in the head by a kickball while I sat on the ground, reading. The ball bounced off me, and I resumed my place in the book. There was also the time a classmate invited me to his birthday party. "But you can't bring a book," he told me. Bump that. When I was about eleven or twelve years old, I spent a summer in the Dominican Republic with a heavy video camera on my shoulder, obsessively filming my parents, my brother, aunts, uncles, and cousins. Months after completing graduate school, I spent a few weekends walking around Upper Manhattan for a series I created about its residents for a hyperlocal blog. I interviewed people and wrote tiny vignettes based on our conversations, then asked to take their portrait. There was also the short-lived Instagram account where I snapped photos of discarded shoes and sandals and invented stories around how they ended up in these mean streets. All this to say, I have unwittingly been working toward this book for most of my life.

I would not have been able to write most of this project had I not known Spanish, the language my parents passed down to me. For that I am grateful. As someone who was born in the United States to parents who were born elsewhere, I have this unsettling fear of losing ties to my heritage and to the deep connection I feel to the Dominican Republic. This project may very well be a part of my psyche showing itself. It is a small, full-hearted way for me to preserve my family's story and my heritage. Some memories become lost with time, and I refuse to resign the stories my parents still have, and of others I spoke with for this project, to memory. I committed to reaching beyond that, to arranging them on the page. *Bodega Stories* is a container for these stories. Not all of them, obviously, but enough to hopefully feel the store's heartbeat. Its spirit.

Over the years my parents have worked very hard. They've shared the weight of their bodega. The bills and invoices. The vendors. The employees. The customers. The endless questions that come from every direction, in person, by phone, even on social media. They've hired employees who have come and gone. They've even hired family. My parents are both in their sixties now, and I think about their impending retirement. Whenever I ask either of them when they plan to retire, their answer is always opaque. I can't tell if they know and just refuse to say it out loud. Maybe they really aren't sure. I imagine it's painful to say goodbye to a place you've poured everything into. While I wait for their answer, I figured now was the best time to write this book. At its core, *Bodega Stories* is a love letter to my parents.

FROM QUISQUEYA TO NEW YORK CITY

The Dominican Republic (also known as Quisqueya) is part of the Greater Antilles, a grouping of the larger islands in the Caribbean Sea. It shares a maritime border with Puerto Rico to the east, and a land border with Haiti to the west. By the time Christopher Columbus claimed it for Spain, the land had already been home to the Taíno, the Indigenous peoples of the Greater Antilles and surrounding islands. Colonization, forced labor, and diseases brought by Europeans caused the rapid decline in the population of the Taíno people. The Spanish later brought Africans they enslaved to labor in sugarcane plantations, gold mines, and agriculture. Many Dominicans today point to a blend of African, European, and Taíno Indigenous heritage.

Over time, there have been different migration patterns in the Dominican Republic, with distinct root causes. My parents were part of a large wave of Dominicans who migrated to the United States in the second half of the twentieth century. For decades, international travel had been restricted under Rafael Leónidas Trujillo, a notorious dictator who came to power in 1930 and would rule the country for three decades. Passport applications at the time were costly, and the government routinely denied passports even to those who could afford it.

Trujillo's regime was marked by brutality and oppression. He had dissenters followed, imprisoned, tortured, and killed. In the fall of 1937, he ordered the Dominican military to execute Haitians who lived near the DR-Haiti border region. The Parsley Massacre claimed the lives of thousands of Haitian men, women, and children. Among those killed were also Dominicans of Haitian descent. Trujillo tried, unsuccessfully, to have Venezuela's President Rómulo Betancourt assassinated with a car bomb. He also had three well-regarded sisters murdered: Patria, Minerva, and María Teresa Mirabal, known as Las Mariposas (the Butterflies), were activists, part of a growing underground resistance in DR against Trujillo's dictatorship.

On May 30, 1961, six months after the murders of Las Hermanas Mirabal, Trujillo was assassinated while on his way to San Cristobal in a Chevrolet driven by his chauffeur. A group of men ambushed him on a lonely stretch of highway. "The only way to get rid of him was to kill him," Antonio Imbert Barrera, a military officer and one of the men who plotted the assassination, told the BBC in a 2011 interview. After Trujillo's assassination, travel restrictions relaxed for Dominicans and the price of passports dropped. The lines for visa applications stretched on and on.

My father was born in 1962, the year after Trujillo was assassinated, and my mother in 1963. The decades that followed marked a period of political and economic turmoil for the Dominican Republic, which led to more Dominicans looking outside the country for stability. The United States' enactment of the Immigration and Nationality Act of 1965, which overhauled America's immigration system and prioritized family reunification, cracked the door even wider for Dominicans to migrate to the US. Many settled in New York City, where they opened businesses to earn a living: beauty salons, restaurants, barbershops, taxi service companies, bodegas.

Papi left DR for New York because his Tío Bobito, the younger brother of my Abuela Rosa Julia, needed people he could trust to work at his bodega in Brooklyn. *But I really had no plans to come to New York,* my father tells me.

Mami was one of ten siblings in a middle-class family from El Cibao, a region located in the northern part of DR. She was still a child when some of her older siblings began migrating to the US, settling into new lives across the boroughs of NYC. By fourteen, she was in Brooklyn. When I ask Ma why she migrated here, she tells me what I have heard many people say. Un mejor futuro. She came here for a better future.

Decades later, Dominicans are now considered the largest immigrant group in New York City. They have also carved out a significant presence in other states like New Jersey, Massachusetts, and Pennsylvania. Many others have left the cold of the Northeast for a sunnier state. Like my family, they ended up calling Florida home.

FREDDY AND DAMARIS CASTILLO AT A CONCERT IN THE DOMINICAN REPUBLIC.

"LA GUACHERNA"

In the beginning there was Brooklyn. The second youngest of five girls in the Taveras family, Mami had a strict father. My Abuelo Julito was old school and, because he was old school, Mami's friend had to ask him for permission for my mom to attend a party. The planned gathering was for the wife of one of Papi's tíos. It was a despedida, a farewell party of sorts, because the couple was retiring to DR. But Mami didn't know they were related to Freddy. *I didn't even know Freddy,* my mother shares. *I knew his tío's wife, but I didn't know Freddy.*

Mami, eighteen years old at the time, was single. She had a group of girlfriends, most of whom were dating. *I told one, "You and I are the only ones who are going to be there without a boyfriend." And she tells me, "Oh no, I have a boyfriend now." And I thought to myself, "Bueeeno, I'm going to be the only single one there then."* The memory still makes her laugh. Abuelo Julito agreed to let his daughter attend. With the official green light from her father, Damaris's excitement grew. She went out and bought an outfit for the party. A red dress, a new pair of shoes.

The day arrived, and rain began to pour in their corner of Brooklyn. *And my papá tells me, "Ay Damaris, it's raining. You can't go to that party,"* she recalls. *I said, "Oh no! I already bought my vestidito and my zapaticos!" In those days you didn't buy many new clothes.* Abuelo thankfully didn't push back.

Damaris's brother, Domingo, picked her up to escort her to the party. He didn't stay long. As for Mami, she did her thing. She mingled and enjoyed herself. Later that night, Jose, another of Damaris's brothers, swung by to pick her up and escort her home. *My brother, Jose, was very affectionate,* Damaris says, *so he hugged me.* It takes time and several rounds of goodbyes to properly leave a Dominican party, so brother and sister would end up staying a while.

When Freddy arrived at the gathering, he noticed a young woman seated with a guy beside her. She was beautiful. *I thought, "Wow, que linda 'ta. Esa muchacha me gusta."* He knew right away that he liked her.

Damaris felt the same sparks when she saw Freddy—tall and slim, but built. *From the moment your papá entered that party, I said, "Ohmaigah. This muchacho is interestante." I thought he was handsome. I had never seen him before.* She chuckles again.

Freddy saw the gorgeous girl, then focused on the guy next to her. How this man had his arm around the girl. Freddy assumed they were a couple. *So I asked one of my cousins, Henry, I said, "Henry, I like that girl, pero mira, she has a boyfriend."*

Henry looked over to see who Freddy was scoping out. El primo saw it was Damaris. They went to high school together. Henry knew Damaris, and he knew her family. So Henry knew that his cousin was mistaken. He cleared things right up, Papi remembers. *Henry told me, "No. That's her brother."*

Upon hearing that, Freddy felt a wave of relief. He thought, *There's hope for me yet.* He learned her name was Damaris.

Later, he found the right moment to ask Damaris in the red dress for a dance. The song they danced to, he remembers, was "La Guacherna" by Milly y Los Vecinos. A lively merengue. Afterward, he asked for her number. Damaris gave it to him. It was the number for her house phone. He called the following day. And their story began.

THIS IS WHERE

The entrance to Orlando Latin Market is an aluminum frame double door, but only the right one is used. This is where people hold the door open for you, sometimes, but where everyone steps aside for the doña ambling by with her cart. Where people complain about the immigration system, the increasingly heavy traffic, the overall cost of living, government bureaucracy. Where men ogle at women's bodies or sneak in glances. Where others avert their gaze. Here, víveres—starchy root vegetables like yuca, boniato, yautía—are sold by the pound. Many customers come here seeking traces of the countries they left behind, but never *really* left behind, because the countries they were born into are always in their hearts. Sometimes, these same countries may cause a phantom artery blockage. Chest pain, tightness, shortness of breath. Homesickness hurts. The bodega is where a man looks for a gasket ring for his mother's greca because, without it, she can't make her café. And who are we as a society without our coffee? Where people come in asking if we sell cigarettes. We don't. Where customers risk damaging the aguacates by squeezing them too hard. Not all press their thumbs into the avocados, but some can't help it because they're not trying to pay for something that is rotten inside. Here you'll find sazón (spice blend seasoning), and verbal seasoning if you don't come correct. Where some customers smile, amused, at the Cuban and Dominican women behind the register talking loudly. And where others appear uncomfortable, like they've walked into a party where they don't know anyone. Where the owner, Freddy, blows into a paper bag, squeezes it closed, and pops it behind the cashier, Liuba, and his sister-in-law, Margarita, to scare them. This is where people navigate around language barriers. Where some customers point to steaming hot foods from behind the glass covering because they can't speak Spanish and the workers are still learning English. There is a lot of pointing. Where people sometimes complain about the prices to the owners, employees, anyone who will listen. Unfortunately, if the cost goes up for the bodeguero, it is felt by the customer. Where, at the register, men and women let out audible sighs because they are ground down by work and by life. Like Dominicans say, en la lucha. In the struggle. In the fight. People arrive here with bright smiles, shy smiles, or polite smiles. Others step in con la cara amarga—their problems and worries carving bitter scowls out of their faces. This is where customers grab a basket from the stack next to the register, their eyes already focused on their destined aisle. Where people talk about elections back in their native countries, and where they fire against corrupt politicians both there and in the good ol' USA. Where you can find packaged ajonjolí acaramelado, sesame brittle, and maní acaramelado, peanut brittle. Where former employees still shop from time to time. Where people yell at each other from across the store, but they're truly just talking. Where a customer speaks to my mother in a condescending tone. Where exchanging pleasantries means asking each other about your children and your aging parents in one endless loop. Where most people pay with cash, card, coins, EBT, and where a few have risked felony charges by attempting to use counterfeit money. Where a sick man caresses the face of a young cashier, in front of his wife. In walk deeply flawed humans, wounded humans, humans in pain. This is where some longtime customers come in ready to spar jovially with the owner, Freddy. Where they joke with him and vice versa. Where hardened, round stomachs shake from a good laugh. Where people catch an attitude. Where a young cashier tends to two women at the register who complain loudly about how they can get these ingredients cheaper elsewhere. But they still buy the items. And after they leave, the cajera hides in the bathroom and cries. People come here asking for limoncillos, or quenepas, or mamoncillos, or Spanish limes, or chenets . . . whatever you call them. This is where, after paying, some customers stand off to the side to study their receipts because they want to make sure they weren't charged twice for an item. Where a cancer survivor shares the wonderful news that he's in remission. Where an older man stands at the checkout counter, wanting to pay already, but his wife is still off to the side trying to get more things. Where owner Damaris plays old boleros on Bluetooth and belts out the lyrics, sometimes off-key. Where customers still buy international calling cards to connect with their loved ones back home. And where customers turned close friends of the owners sit behind the register to shoot the shit because they feel at home. Orlando Latin Market is where people delight in finding a product from their country—El Salvador, Colombia, Peru, Mexico, Ecuador, Honduras. Where people arrive in their Sunday best to pick up food or something sweet after church services. Where two Black boys in checkered button-down shirts and slacks stop in with their elders, then laugh with each other about something funny on the way out. Where a Cuban woman has to rein in her toddler from straying too far from her in the store. Where you can find dulce de leche y guayaba, rectangular-shaped milk creams attached to reddish-brown slabs of guava paste. So good. Where a man successfully pays for items with a fake twenty-dollar bill. Where construction workers—their hands coated by dust and dirt—file in together for some hot food on their lunch breaks. Where the same word in Spanish will have different meanings depending on what country you hail from, causing embarrassment or misunderstanding (look up *papaya*). Where people voice their opinions, or withhold them. Where they regret the past, or refuse to look back. Here there are gorditos, flaquitos, llenitas, y delgaditas. Orlando Latin Market is where Puerto Ricans come in search of parchment paper, banana leaves, and balls of twine, all must-haves for their pasteles. Where Salvadorans come for the cheese they need to make plump pupusas at home. In the back aisle, below the detergents and bars of soap, you'll find rows of candles. We have seven-day candles for your spiritual needs. Others depict saints. A barefoot San Judas Tadeo, Jude the Apostle, with a flame above his head. Santa Bárbara, the patron saint of miners, artillerymen, architects, and anyone working with explosives. San Martín de Porres, who was born in Peru and is considered the first Black saint in the Americas, is on yet another candle looking stoic. We also can't forget the Divino Niño with his golden hair and arms stretched out to the sky. This is where professional baseball players get a taste of home. If they're Dominican peloteros, they come for plátanos, salchichón, and Country Club soda.

This is where pot-bellied old men greet you by commenting on how much weight you've gained. The irony is ironclad. Where you can indulge your sweet tooth with Cuban sponrru bizcochos—spongy cakes cut into long, thin rectangles. Here they also sell boniatillos made from boniato—each tropical sweet potato mound held in a baking cup. And on scorching summer days, you can cool off with a creamy Mamita's popsicle. Orlando Latin Market is where some over-the-counter medicines have aggressive ass names, like Rompe Pecho, a cough syrup that basically translates to "Break Chest." Here you'll find coffee, canned sardines, oatmeal, breadcrumbs, yellow cherries in jars, figs in syrup, big cooking pots, frozen oxtail, plastic piggy banks, and tomato paste for your stewed beans. And here you can call and ask if they carry something else we haven't mentioned. This is where Freddy and Damaris share laughs and sometimes disagree. Where this couple, married for decades, choose each other and their business day after day after day.

BULLETIN BOARD IN JANUARY

Efficiency Apartments and Used Shoes

Outside Orlando Latin Market, to the right of the metal merchandiser with bags of ice, is a bulletin board for anyone from the community wanting to put up a notice or ad. My father installed it years ago. Above the board, mounted to the store's brick exterior, is a wooden parrot the color of seafoam. Its globular-shaped eyes appear to watch over all who have something to advertise, or those who simply want to look. On any given day you may see a customer peering through the plastic covering, reading the collection of notices held down by an assortment of colorful or clear pushpins. Most are handwritten in Spanish. Some days, you may see a few customers huddled around the board. The door to the community bulletin is locked. Access can only be granted with a key you request from the employees behind the register counter. There's a lock now because the wind used to fling the doors open, sending slips of paper flying.

By the way, are you looking for a place to live? There are plenty of efficiency apartments available for rent around here. A small paper ripped from a spiral notepad reads, "Se renta efficiency en Largo todo incluido." An efficiency for rent in Largo, with everything included. An 8x11 sheet of paper has a damn near dissertation about an "hermoso efficiency"—a gorgeous efficiency with a walk-in closet, private entrance, and central AC. But there are no pets allowed, so you can't bring your Rocky, Brooklyn, Lola, Teddy, Ace, or Chewy. And you can forget about smoking. That's not allowed either. Another flyer, pinned horizontally, has a straightforward message. In bold red and all caps, it reads: SE ALQUILA UN CUARTO. ROOM FOR RENT. It includes a St. Petersburg address and a number to call if interested. A few more ads for efficiency rentals are dotted throughout the bulletin, under pushpins.

There are fewer than a handful of business cards that offer something different. A taxi service. An experienced mobile auto repair guy for your brake needs. A home remodeling contractor.

To las mujeres: Do you have old shoes that you'd like to get rid of, but feel guilty about throwing away? How about those chestnut gladiator sandals that you wore that one time? Remember you thought it'd be cute to look like you came straight out the Colosseum. Or those aquamarine slingback pumps that you wore down to smithereens? And those red stilettos. Oh yeah, the uncomfortable stilettos you were so excited about 'cause you were going to stunt at the club, but then proceeded to whine and complain about all night. Well, apparently there's someone who buys used women's shoes and wants you to text them if you have any. Can't promise this person will actually want your raggedy pairs, but reach out anyway to see.

A CONVERSATION WITH PAPI

AMARIS: OK, Pa, so I'm writing this book about you, about Mami, about your bodega. What do you think about me writing this book?

PAPI: That's good. So readers can know what certain people go through in the bodega and all that. There are some who think that being a bodeguero is simply being behind a counter, checking out. But it's not like that. There are a lot of things wrapped up in being a bodeguero.

AMARIS: Like what?

PAPI: Oh! Being a bodeguero means you're in accounting. You have to buy merchandise. You have to work with employees—if one is sick, or if another didn't show up. All those things. It's not easy.

AMARIS: I know it's not easy. I see that you're tired.

PAPI: Sí, pero hay que seguir pa'lante, porque imagínate. Hay que seguirle dando patadita' a la latita [Yes, but you have to keep going, because imagine. You have to keep kicking the can].

AMARIS: [Laughs] La patita' a la latita?

PAPI: *Patadita'* a la latita.

AMARIS: Patadita' a la latita. And there's also the customers.

PAPI: Yes. We're lucky that 99 percent of customers, I would say, are good people. Good customers. But sometimes there appears one who tries to make your life impossible. But you know how to manage the situation. What you do is, you breathe in deeply, and let it go.

AMARIS: Very deeply, right? [Laughs]

PAPI: Yes. You breathe in deeply and you let it go. Because you're not going to sour your life over one person.

AMARIS: It's true. Like Mami says, *You have to use la psicología.*

PAPI: Many times, you have to be a hypocrite. Sometimes.

AMARIS: Ay ay ay. But I love many of your customers. You have good people.

PAPI: Sí, sí. We have a really good clientele.

AMARIS: And what I really like about your bodega is that you enter and you feel . . . I have always said this: You feel like you're in a different country when you enter. Or different countries.

PAPI: Not only that. Every day there are people who tell us, *Ay, I love coming to this bodega because here you breathe in an air of happiness, of peace, de alegría.* It's true. Sometimes I tell the muchachas who serve the food, I tell them, *Dios mío, this is like a gallinero* [*a henhouse*]. There's one who laughs like a brujita.

AMARIS: [Laughs]

PAPI: And one day I told her, *You know, I thought of you last night.* And she asked, *Why, Freddy?* And I said, *I was watching a movie and out came a witch who laughed just like you do.*

AMARIS: And what did she say?

PAPI: She exploded with laughter.

AMARIS: [Laughs] Oh, man.

LA CAJA

previous THE CASH REGISTER AT ORLANDO LATIN MARKET.

THE TEA

Sleeplessness brings Deborah here on a Saturday afternoon. She stops by the register counter, her petite frame easily fitting into the gap reserved for employees—between the plastic bag stand and the tall shelf carrying bottles of castor oil and domino sets. She is dressed in a light blue, button-down shirt and olive pants. Her hair—white and chin-length—is part Hollywood waves and part June's mugginess. She leans forward and attempts to say something in Spanish to the women by the register. "Flore? Linden?"

Deborah is in search of linden tea. Mami offers to show her where it's located. The customer and I follow her. We make a left, then another left until the three of us are standing before the shelves lined with tea. There the cartons are, lined up and stacked neatly, mostly. Here are teas of different kinds. Prune, ginger & turmeric, guanabana. Most carry promises in two languages:

Aids digestion—Ayuda a la digestión.
Immune booster—Inmunizador.
Natural antioxidant—Antioxidante natural.

Mami points to where the linden teas are.

"Is this it?" I ask Deborah. "Linden? Linden leaves?"

The woman studies the boxes.

"They have so many teas," I point out. "Oh, linden flowers."

Gesturing to two different linden tea boxes, Mami explains, "It's the same thing, but different company." She points to the Badia brand.

Deborah chooses a white box containing twenty-five bags of linden tea. In Spanish, it's té de tilo. A cornflower-blue banner near the bottom declares the tea to be a soothing relaxant. The customer thanks us and approaches la caja, the cash register. Places the carton on the conveyor belt, then a folded dollar bill and a coin atop the box. She declines a paper bag for her purchase.

Outside the store, Deborah says she hopes this will help her. She plans to try the linden tea tonight before bed. “A Mexican doctor told me to get this to sleep better. He said, *Take linden.*”

Deborah doesn’t speak Spanish, but she is a lover of languages and admits to shooting from the hip when she walked into the bodega to try to ask about tea en español. Deborah believes it’s a courtesy to try to speak to someone in their native language. “You come into a Hispanic grocery store, you might at least say, *Permiso.*” Deborah tells me she couldn’t find this tea at the other places she tried. Says she came here because this is a Hispanic market. “You want to find a Hispanic thing, you go where the real deal is.”

A (RE)PROPOSAL

From behind la caja, the cushioned chair creaks underneath her weight. Damaris is tired and needs to sit for a bit. Today she's wearing a purple shirt and leggings under her thin plastic apron, the same worn by the cubanas who tend to customers wanting hot food. Her short coarse hair, in highlights, is pulled back into a ponytail.

Just then, her husband approaches her. Freddy has been waiting for this moment. Damaris looks up at him. Then down at his hands.

"What?"

Freddy kneels down in front of her. He smiles. His eyes glint with playfulness. He's holding something circular and blue. A ring. Damaris smiles, too, as he reaches for her right hand. She turns toward him to make room for whatever he's about to say. Or ask. Her apron crinkles and stretches underneath their bridged hands.

"I don't have the money to buy you a real ring, mi amor," Freddy says, his voice coated in affection. "But the intention is what counts." He places the ring on his wife's right middle finger. Her real ring finger is already occupied.

"Ay, gracias," Damaris says, her thank-you lilting in volume. Freddy positions it just right on her brown hand. Her smile stretches wider. What he gifted her is a tamper-evident ring—what's usually left on a bottle after you unscrew the cap.

One of the cashiers, Dailin, cheers for the couple. Freddy chuckles and stands up to continue his work. This is not the first time he has proposed to his wife. Not the first time he's taken items and fashioned them into jewelry. Many times before, he has peeled the gold foil from a Modelo beer bottle and shaped it into a ring. And each time, he offers it to his wife. A renewed proposal. Honeyed déjà vu. A moment of sweetness after decades of marriage.

Dailin encourages her boss to show off her anillo de compromiso—her engagement ring. Still beaming, Damaris wiggles her hand. The happy wife then removes the ring to inspect it. Holds it in her left hand before placing it back on her finger.

"Wow," she says, looking up again at her husband. "Qué romántico."

I was not a witness to this proposal. But Dailin recorded the moment on her phone and sent me the video. When I open my WhatsApp to the message, I watch my mother in her purple shirt and white apron, my father kneeling before her. The moment is equal parts amusing, moving, and funny. My lips stretch on their own. Wide, so wide they stick to my teeth. That there are still moments of sweetness between them after decades of marriage is remarkable. I send Dailin back three laughing emojis with tears spilling from their faces.

"Gracias por compartir," I write. I thank her for sending me this moment. Then I deliver a red heart emoji that palpitates.

That's love.

EYES ON THE PRIZE

Agustín holds the plastic produce bag in his left hand and sorts through plátanos with his right. The green plantains—priced at 2 x $1.00—are piled into a cardboard box lined in thin plastic, between bunches of culantro and plump burro bananas. "La abuela makes them chicharritas," the eighty-seven-year-old explains. He's referring to his wife, who sent him on this errand. She will use what he buys today to prepare lunch for two of their grandchildren. Chicharritas are thinly sliced plantains that are fried. Agustín's family is at home, waiting for him to return with the goods.

Today he is dressed in a light blue-gray button-down and gray slacks with brown shoes. His cell phone is tucked away in his chest pocket in case his wife calls in need of something more. Agustín studies the plátanos with a keen eye, digging for the ones he deems the most suitable. He plucks one from the pile and moves it over to the right. He had been instructed to get three. He pulls one out from the pile and slides it into the bag. "They ask for tostones," he shares of his grandchildren. "How they love them." Now his hands dig deeper. He pulls out one plantain and quickly abandons it. Bends his head forward a bit and peers into the box. His hands glide against the tough skin of several plátanos until he grabs hold of one near the bottom of the box. As he pulls, the others rub against each other. They rumble like thunder as they rise and fall. Agustín then drops the final green plantain into the thin bag. The retiree turns around and steps to la caja just feet away. The cash register's screen displays the total: $1.50. He pays in cash, receives his change, and slips the future meal into a black grocery bag.

El don was only able to drive on this Wednesday in June because his eyes are healthier. Cataracts had begun to cloud Agustín's vision, so he had them removed. "Yo tengo seguro bueno, que no tengo que pagar ni un kilo." Says he's got good insurance from his old job—so good that he didn't have to pay anything for the surgery. He adds, "I thought they were going to take away my driver's license." La licencia de conducir, de manejar is something many take for granted. Agustín stresses those last words in Spanish, elongating them. The prospect of losing the privilege to drive is alarming, especially in a place like Florida. Cars drive through the state's veins all day, every day, and every which way. Agustín says he's been driving in the United States for about twenty-four years. Says he's never had a fine. There was one time, he admits, when he was stopped while on the road after drinking a few beers.

At his age, Agustín has a clinic he goes to specifically for eye exams. All he has to do is pick up the phone to schedule an appointment. Recently he received an order to appear with his driver's license in hand. It was up for renewal, and the state of Florida needed to ensure he was still fit for the road. Aloud, Agustín reasons that they have a right to do that. He says someone who has just had eye surgery should not be free to possibly cause an accident. He decided he wanted to stay on the road. So he took the necessary steps. Had his eyes checked. "They put an apparatus over here," Agustín says, gesturing to his eyes. He remembers the woman conducting the exam saying, *Ohhh.* His voice slopes up at the end. Perhaps the woman was surprised. He recalls handing her a card from his clinic. "They told me that my eyesight is, until this moment, perfect."

He thought his driver's license would maybe be renewed for one year, maybe two. "When they did all that to me, the muchacha tells me, *Mira, we're going to renew you for five more years. Here's your license.*" Agustín laughs with unbridled joy as he recounts the story.

Some people had told him to lay low. They warned Agustín, said he'd have his license taken away because of his age. Because of his eyes. But Agustín maintains he was never afraid. "No," he assures, probably to himself. "De verdad. You won't get anything if you let fear take over."

BACHATA AND BOLERO

Music didn't always play consistently here. It was never a guarantee that you'd enter and hear Antony Santos lamenting about how he fell in love with a woman. "El Mayimbe" of bachata was resistant to el amor, and now he couldn't explain how it all went down. Nor could you walk in and always be met with the percussive spirits of Gloria Estefan's "Mi Tierra" reviving the dead, or the late, great Celia Cruz urging us in song to live our lives. But that all changed once my mother learned to use a Bluetooth speaker.

One morning in mid-September, Mami connects her phone to her speaker from behind the register counter. Searches on YouTube and settles on a playlist.

"Quién es esa?" a man, hearing the first song, asks my mom. "Quién es esa, Damaris?" The customer wants to know the name of the woman whose voice now bellows from the speaker.

"Yolandita Monge," Damaris replies. "She's Puerto Rican."

The song playing is "Cierra los Ojos y Juntos Recordemos." It was a hit in the Dominican Republic and in many other countries. In the song, Monge comes across an old love. She asks that they close their eyes and remember.

"Oh, that's too far back," the man tells my mom. "I was still a boy when she sang." The customer jokes that he was still a baby who didn't yet listen to music. Laughing, Ma tells him and the cashier that they're jovencitos. They're too young to know about this music, about this singer. Seconds later, she sings along with the international star.

My mom learned how to use Bluetooth from the women at work. It was a process. If she's stuck or has questions, she has no problem asking. "I ask everyone. Customers—a todo el mundo." At first, it was difficult for her to catch on. "Pero uno aprende todo en la vida," she tells me. One can learn anything in life. At the store, Damaris plays music across genres. Boleros, bachata, salsa, merengue. Her favorite genres are bachata and bolero, best known for their lyrics about love and heartbreak.

A few minutes later, my mother retrieves her cell phone from the shelf and clicks on a different YouTube video. Another woman's voice drips in melancholy. The store hums. Music plays for a while. Less than ten minutes later, Damaris picks up her phone again. She holds it in her left hand and scrolls through songs on the playlist with her right pointer finger. Clicks on a song, but it does not play. "What happened?" she asks, mostly to herself.

"Leo Dan? 'Tú Me Pides Que Te Olvide'?" I ask. "But you just played that one." Annoyed, Mami continues scrolling. Tells me she got this.

LA SOLEDAD NO MATA

Whenever my Tía Margarita works, she does so restlessly. She's got an eye for presentation. She lines up canned goods in tidy rows, prices packaged desserts and stacks each neatly on top of the other in the fridge. She washes this. Picks up that. Within my aunt is a deep urgency for order. I have childhood memories of family gatherings at her old house on Long Island, and how clean and orderly she kept it. My aunt has a decades-long itch to clean and to keep her surroundings immaculate.

On a Saturday afternoon in late July, Margarita drags the wastebasket from the front kitchen and down the aisle, past the packaged arepas de choclo and gallons of milk. She turns right, then makes another sharp right until she's standing before handmade wooden shelves painted green. On the shelves, cardboard boxes display piles of boniato, yautía, and yuca—long and tapered with waxy, brown skin. There are bags of dry red beans and cornmeal that can fit in your palm. A swath of earthly tones. Margarita places a yellow-orange rag at the thin ledge where two cardboard boxes meet, and her hands begin their work.

It is shortly before 2 p.m. The bodega's soundtrack is a collective of voices and laughter. By the front kitchen, customers list their meat and starch of choice to the women who serve food in white containers. Employees joke and speak among each other with the warmth that can only come from hours on their feet together. Accents and dialects interweave or clash. From her aisle, Tía tunes it all out. She is hyperfocused on two boxes of yellow onions. She picks up the edible jumbo-sized bulbs from the box on the left and drops them in the box beside it. Once she has moved over a handful of onions, she finds what she's looking for on the left box's flat bottom: pieces of tunic, translucent and flaky, that have come off the onions.

You go to the supermarket, she'll tell me later, *and the first impression is what you see.* And Margarita really cares about first impressions. She works swiftly, raking the detached skins with her gloved fingers and dropping them into the trash bin. "I'm cleaning the onions a bit. Tú sabe," she explains. "Organizing a bit here." Once Margarita is done clearing out the first box of tunics, she places the onions back in their rightful spot. She then turns her attention to some red onions. Plucks some loose skins from their box, too.

At the end of the aisle, two women go over their shopping list. My aunt greets them. "Hola, cómo están?" She tells them what she's doing.

"That's good," the woman closest to Margarita says approvingly. "Because if not, they go bad."

—

My Tía Margarita has worked part time at Orlando Latin Market for years. If she isn't in the kitchen filling to-go containers with hot food, she is up front by the register as the cashier's right hand. Here she is on Saturdays and Sundays, bagging groceries and fielding a nonstop trickle of questions from customers.

Wherever my aunt is, expect a hint of glamour. I'm talking everywhere. For one, she never steps foot inside the bodega without lipstick. Her dyed blonde hair is usually pulled in an updo—each strand sprayed into submission. Her work uniform is by her own design: a form-fitting patterned top with fitness leggings, and sneakers, which are a must so she can be quick on her feet at the store.

I begin our interview by stating the obvious. "You're known in our family for always looking well put together." A small laugh slips from my tía's magenta-colored lips. In Spanish, I ask her: "Why are you this way?"

This is who she is, ever since she was younger—más jovencita—in New York. "I have always been like this because it boosts my self-esteem, and it makes me feel better," she says nonchalantly. For Margarita, taking care of her appearance is the key to feeling good, and she insists people need to feel good about themselves.

My aunt acknowledges she's no longer jovencita, but her pride in her appearance remains the same. There is a formula to her self-love. It starts in the morning, when she prepares herself a green smoothie made from water, cucumber, lime, un diente de ajo (a garlic clove), spinach,

TÍA MARGARITA POSES
IN ORLANDO LATIN MARKET.

pineapple, and a bit of ginger. She remembers to take her biotin and collagen supplements. *I don't have headaches,* she told me once. *People don't believe it, but it's true.* Says she thanks God, every day, for her health. She also works out three days a week—Monday, Tuesday, and Wednesday—and takes group classes followed by a forty-five-minute walk on the treadmill. She never goes to sleep with foundation on. Night cream before bed is a must. And she always, *always* feeds her hands, feet, and arms with moisturizing lotion. If Margarita goes out, she first applies sunscreen, then makeup. If she's staying at home, then just sunscreen will do. But if she's going to the bodega? Then makeup is required. In fact, she applies color to her lips even if just to take out the garbage. She's always in either sandals or small heels, and she only switches to sneakers for the store and the gym. She usually arrives at the bodega in platform chanclas, then slips into sneakers.

I ask Tía Margarita how she would describe her current style. She tells me, "A señora who is seventy-one years old, but has the spirit and energy of about forty-five years old." A hearty laughter erupts from her mouth as soon as she says it. I find the specificity of forty-five hilarious, so I laugh with her. "Age, as they say, is a number, really," she informs me. "Because I have a lot of energy. And I feel good. I feel young. I feel a desire to work, to be active, to go to the gym. To do everything."

The Sunshine State has been home to Tía Margarita for more than two decades. She left New York after she and her husband divorced. At that time, my aunt says she yearned for distance. She was desperate to be far from New York, far from anyone who could probe about what happened in the marriage. She felt a big move was the best move. "You know how people are," she says flatly. "They'll ask the same questions."

In Florida, Margarita began life anew. She moved in with us and took up the smallest bedroom meant for my brother. She searched for a new Hispanic church and learned about St. Cecelia Catholic Church in Clearwater. She began attending Mass there. "I clung to God so He would help me," she remembers.

In time, Margarita made new friends. She found community at the store and got to know people from different countries. They arrive at the store and bring her their questions and problems, and she tries to help them. She says she cherishes the exchange of cultures, the seesaw of conversations. Here, Margarita developed a new rhythm. Stayed with it. And she never remarried. "I feel good like this—sola," she declares. "I've gotten used to it. Y hago lo que me de la gana." Says she does what she wants. Tía Margarita once heard that women are better able to choose the best partner when they enjoy being alone without feeling bad for themselves. "Because if you're scared of solitude, you accept whatever appears before you," she cautions, "to have company." Margarita now indulges in la soledad. Yes, she spends time with friends. Yes, she catches up with them on occasion over lunch. But she always relishes the return home alone. "Perhaps that's why I haven't had a partner, because I really like solitude," she offers. My aunt sounds confident when she says this, clear-eyed in her self-assessment.

What if, perhaps tomorrow, or in the near future, or years from now, someone enters Margarita's orbit? What if they give her the space she's grown accustomed to? According to her, that hasn't happened yet.

Over the years, I watched men at the bodega try to woo my aunt. They were attracted to her beautiful face, her high energy, and how she carries herself with enviable self-confidence. Or maybe it was something else that drew them to her. There have been attempts to court her in the different spaces of her daily life. At gatherings hosted by mutual friends, in Bible study groups at church.

In response, Margarita admits to lying many times. She tells them she has a boyfriend. "I've had many suitors," she says. "But none qualify."

Laughter shoots out of her. A carefree sound, without a rigid frame.

WORKING WITH DINOSAURS

One January day, an older white man with rounded rectangle eyeglasses enters Orlando Latin Market. It is Buck. In his hand is a black plastic bag. There is nothing special about the bag. It's a regular T-shirt bag. But it contains a few things the store needs.

Buck greets Freddy, who is standing behind the register. Buck is a distributor in the label printing business. He travels often for work. Most of his business is in wholesale. But on this Wednesday, Buck finds time before another business trip to return a few items that belong to my father. He stands off to the side of the counter, in front of the stack of baskets. He places the bag on the slanted metal counter.

"Here are your guns," Buck says, pulling three old school retail price guns from the bag. Buck had stopped by Orlando Latin Market a few days prior, when Papi asked him to check all the bodega's price guns. Buck found three bad ones, each with various broken parts that had to be repaired. Today, Buck is returning the guns, now back in working order. He shows them to Freddy and demonstrates that they are fine now.

In exchange, Freddy gives him fifty dollars. Ten more than what Buck expects. A tip.

"Thank you, but I—" Buck says.

"No problem," Freddy replies.

"I don't—"

"It's OK," Freddy assures him.

"No, no, no. I don't take—"

Papi again cuts him off.

"It's OK."

"No, no, no. Come on, Freddy—"

"It's OK, man," Pa says. "Yeah, man."

"I mean, OK," Buck says finally. "Thank you. Appreciate it. Do you need a ticket?"

The bodeguero says no. He doesn't need one. He thanks Buck.

"Take care," Buck says. He tells Freddy that he can call him anytime.

Buck began working with Freddy a year ago through a mutual connection. Freddy would hand any price guns that needed fixing to his friend, who would pass them over to Buck. The mutual friend eventually sold his business and, when he did, asked Buck to continue to take care of Freddy. Repairing the retail guns is not difficult. "Takes a minute or two. I mean, you got to take a part off the front and loosen two screws and pull it off, and then you gotta put the nose roller back in," he explains to me. "To fix two of those guns probably took ten minutes apiece." The other took seconds.

Buck's repair job is more of a side gig. And when he does repairs, they're always on price guns. Buck likens price guns to "dinosaur-like equipment" because they're not as popular anymore with businesses. These days, more and more people use scanning through barcodes. At their bodega, my parents scan many items at the register. But there are other items that have the small neon orange stickers with prices stamped on them in black ink, made possible by the price guns.

Buck has been in this industry for more than four decades. He's worked for two leading manufacturers and is now an independent master distributor. "Most of my business is wholesale," he explains. "I deal with mostly wholesalers who supply and support the convenience store trade. That's where the volume of labels is—the volume of guns. Wholesalers buy cases of labels and the full case of twenty guns at a time. That's my business."

He doesn't have too many stores like Orlando Latin Market that he works with. "Today, as people go more to scanning and less to labeling, it's like fishing. You want to go fish where people tell you there's fish," he says. "It doesn't do any good today to go into an auto parts retail, 'cause nobody there has used any price guns in the past twenty years."

Buck says Freddy was kind to give him that tip. He tried to hand the bodeguero the two five-dollar bills back. But Freddy wouldn't accept it. "That doesn't happen very often," Buck says. "What price I charge people is what I'm fine with."

GOD IS EVERYTHING TO ESTHER

Esther can be found every Sunday at GT Church over on Seventeenth Avenue North. And after service, she can often be found here. She comes to Orlando Latin Market mainly for one thing: chicharrones. Consisting of fried pork belly or fried pork rinds, the chicharrón is very popular. In the back kitchen, heaps of it are deep-fried daily and brought over in metal trays to the hot food display out front. They're placed in Styrofoam to-go containers with rounded edges, sold by the pound. Esther doesn't pair the chicharrones with fried yuca, nor does she chop them up to use as a topping for scrambled eggs or black beans. "I just love them alone, watch TV, and crunch on them. And fight my daughter for them," she says with a laugh.

One Sunday in mid-March, Esther arrives at the store in a great mood fresh after service. A short dark brown bob frames her kind face, and her ears are adorned with big silver hoops. She wears a black T-shirt that hugs her curvaceous figure. The front of it reads, in white: I LOVE MY CHURCH. The back of the shirt reads GOD in bold white, along with ADAM, NOAH, ABRAHAM, DAVID. And JESUS of course. The church's logo punctuates the names, near her lower back. Her shoes are also black, and sparkly.

A few other customers are already in front of the hot food display, placing orders. When Esther steps up to the glass covering, her eyes search for the familiar snack. I find it endearing how she pronounces chicharrones. She calls them "cheech-ah-rones." Behind the glass is a metal tray piled high with the fried pork rinds. "Are they burnt?" Esther asks. I can't tell if she's asking me or the workers. I follow her line of sight to see for myself. Most of the meat attached to the pigskin is charred. They appear to have been kept in the fryer too long. One of the employees behind the counter recognizes Esther and knows the customer wants her chicharrones. She uses a pair of tongs to pick the best of the bunch. "Yeah, they are burnt. I love them so much, I guess

I'll go around . . ." Esther says softly to herself or maybe to me, I can't tell. "Maybe they'll give me a discount or something since they got burnt. Yeah, that's fine. I don't like them burnt." Still, she accepts the container of deep-fried pork and orders one tamal. Esther loves hot tamales. "I lived in Miami for a while," she explains, "and I ate *a lot* of Spanish food." Esther then orders one more thing: a pastel de guayaba. She calls it a guava pastel. The jalousie-style pastries are stacked neatly, closest to the glass display.

Esther walks over to wait in line by the register, to pay. Quickly, I circle around the counter and find Papi. I whisper to him, ask if he could grant his regular customer a discount since the chicharrones are a bit burnt. When it is almost Esther's turn at the front of the line, my dad tells her, "No charge."

"No?" she asks. "Oh, thank you."

She opens the container of chicharrones to inspect them again. "I love them so much, I'll close my eyes and eat 'em," she says with a laugh. Esther's total is $3.50, which according to store policy isn't enough to run her debit card. I tell her I will cover it. She thanks me.

I ask Esther to tell me about how she got introduced to Orlando Latin Market. Her son told her about it. "He brought me to this magical place, where I can get my chicharrones, I can get my green tomatoes, I can get hot tamales, I can get guava pastel," she lists. "Things I fell in love with in Miami."

Esther's roots are in the Everglades. She was raised in Belle Glade, a city in south-central Florida that's often referred to as Muck City for its rich soil. After graduation, Esther left for New York at seventeen. She moved around, spending time in Louisiana and Texas before eventually returning to her home state. Her daughter was born here. While in Miami, Esther remembers a Cuban store around the corner from where she lived. "They had everything in 'em. And I ran into chicharrones again," she says. "And he would make them. They'd be long. They would be the long kind. You know, they'd be in a bag and the little meat inside. Oh, they were so good! I can't find that place anymore!" Long story short, she was introduced to Latin food in Miami. So when her

ESTHER POSES WITH A SMILE
IN ORLANDO LATIN MARKET.

son brought her to Orlando Latin Market about five years ago, she was delighted to see some familiar foods. She's also eager to learn to cook some Latin-style dishes herself.

The message she received this Sunday was about God's love. She says her pastor doesn't preach to her and her fellow Christ-followers. He talks with them. Esther says she grew emotional when he and others began praying at the end of service. "I shed some tears, to know that we have so much in our lives to clean up. I'm not perfect. Nobody's perfect. And if you're sitting in church and you think about, *Oh boy, when I get home, I can't wait to have a glass of wine*—I don't think that's sinful, but that's our minds. We gravitate. You can be in church and your mind can be here, or your mind could be, *I got to do this when I go home,* or whatever. And then you'll jerk yourself back and say, *Oh, wait a minute, I better listen.* The Holy Spirit will pull you back when it's time to tell you, *This is something you need to hear.*"

Esther recently encouraged one of her cousins with money troubles to pray without ceasing. "I told her, *You pray all day, every day.* You know. God don't work when we want Him to." As Esther recounts the story, tears begin to well up in her eyes. She says she insisted to her cousin that, when God works, it's right on time.

Esther is now seventy-six years old. She says she no longer gets on her knees to pray because she can hardly get up at her age. "I wouldn't tell anybody, *If you can't get on your knees, don't pray.* Pray anytime, all the time." According to Esther, one of her cousins was having some issues with her stove. She told Esther she smelled gas. Esther urged her to call the gas company. Workers were dispatched. They detected the source of the smell. It was handled. In Esther's eyes, God was behind it all. She remembers telling her cousin that God has His own miraculous ways of saving them. "'And angels . . . It could've been anybody saying, *Come follow me, and I'm going to let you know.* That's the Holy Spirit letting you know there's something going on and you need to correct it. Then you call me. You don't want to check it, but then the Holy Spirit telling me to tell you: *Stop it. Call the electrical people. Call the gas people.* Good thing we did.'"

Esther tells me she doesn't know if she'll ever be good enough to be a missionary, but she knows she can always mention God in her conversations. He means everything to her. "It took me till I got older to see that He has been with me all the time." Her voice trembles. "I can look back on situations that I survived things, or have conquered things, and I've done things. And it couldn't be nobody but God. I've come a long way. Sinful ways when I was young in New York. I did it all." I tell her I have stories too, from my time in New York. "I got stories, but God knows our stories," she tells me. "And I asked for forgiveness."

For years Esther worked as a hospice aide, and before that as a secretary for the Xerox Corporation. And while in Louisiana, she managed a meat market. She is now retired. Up until recently, her sister had been living with her. They were inseparable. Esther says she'd been taking care of her sister, who has Alzheimer's disease, for more than a decade. Her sister now lives with her own daughter in South Florida. On Sundays, Esther and her sister would go to church. After service, they'd come here and get their chicharrones. They'd also take some food to go, for dinner. Maybe they'd go to the park, or visit one of Esther's friends. But sometimes, Esther says, they'd go home and watch Westerns. Her sister loves Westerns. They'd watch *Gunsmoke, The Rifleman, The High Chaparral.* Esther enjoys Westerns, too.

"We old!" she cries. "We watched them when we were kids." Esther says people don't realize how old she is. When she looks in the mirror, she sees her mother, her aunts. At a fair, Esther remembers how her daughter pushed her to participate in that game where a carnival worker guesses people's ages. The man thought Esther was fifty-six. She told him she was seventy-six. He was off by twenty years. She won a prize for him getting her age wrong. It was an alien plushie she ended up giving to one of her great-grandchildren. "I went on about my business," she says. "I was trying to find me a man." Esther has never been married. She says she used to feel sorry for herself because she never got her wedding or her beautiful white dress. She no longer longs for a husband. But a companion would be nice. "I don't even want him to live with me," she insists. "Just enjoy life, go on trips together, fishing. Whatever you do, we'll do. But I don't want to get married."

Esther insists she's got the love of God. She has two children, six grandchildren, and seven great-grandchildren. What she desires most in her life is unity with her family. "I want my family to all love each other. That's what I want. I just want unity and the love of God."

WHERE ARE THE MAMONCILLOS?

The bodega receives many phone calls. There's the occasional scammer telling my parents they're "past due" for the electricity bill, suggesting that they hand over their bank information to avoid getting their power cut off. One time, I was working at the bodega when a caller came in, talking about how we needed to pay a bill. He sounded Dominican, which made me feel especially disappointed. Sometimes it be your own people. When the scammer asked me for our bank's account number, I gave it to him. "Uno, dos, tres, cuatro . . ." He quickly picked up that I was onto him and hung up. *Fuck outta here.*

Most of the time, though, the people calling are real customers with a question. *Are you hiring? Are you accepting pernil orders yet for Nochebuena [Christmas Eve]? Is the yogurt back in stock? Do you carry this very specific thing for this very specific meal I'm making? Is there hot food left?*

The callers speak in English—in different accents and twangs. And in Spanish—in high-speed Spanish, singsong Spanish, unhurried Spanish, struggling Spanish, contemplative Spanish that will try your patience. The questions filter in through the cordless phone positioned above the cash register. On the receiving end of many of these calls is my Tía Margarita. She has a story from one such call. I'll let her tell it:

They called and I answered, "Orlando Latin Market?"

The señor asks me if we have limoncillos. He calls them mamoncillos.

I go, "No, because it's not the season for them. It's in July or August."

And he goes, "OK, so how much are you going to sell it for, per pound?"

And I say, "Señor, how can I tell you how much we're going to sell it for if, one, we don't know if they're going to arrive? And two, we don't know how much it's going to cost us to be able to set a price?"

Imagínate.

And he goes, "Ahh no, because women know everything, I thought you knew."

He told me that.

[Erupts in laughter] *I'm telling you. You hear all kinds of things in this store that you wouldn't believe.*

BULLETIN BOARD IN MARCH

Seeking Roommates and Tabaqueros

There's a lot of ground to cover this month. On a paper ripped from a notepad, someone has written in black marker: "Se RENTA UN MOBILE HOME de 2 cuartos, un baño, cocina, comedor y sala." They're seeking a tenant for a two-room mobile home with a bathroom, kitchen, dining area, and living room. Another notice, on a sun-yellow slip, seeks a renter for a house, four bedrooms, two baths. Call Guillermo.

Do you know how to make cigars? A cigar shop that also serves café would love to have you. The ad reads, in dark red: SE BUSCAN TABAQUEROS. It features an image of an older Black man wearing a panama hat. You can't see his face, but you can see his wrinkled hands expertly rolling a cigar. You can almost smell the cylinder of tobacco—its rich, earthy, almost woody scent. El don knows what he's doing. The flyer also wants you to know: SE PAGA BIEN. They pay well.

Near the top of the board are more slips of paper held down by pushpins—all seeking renters for efficiency apartments. "Se alquila un efice." "Se renta efficcent." "Renta efficient." Each person spells "efficiency" differently. There's also someone looking for a helper who knows about granite. That person should be responsible and want to work. Could that be you? It would be a steady job, you know. Another ad seeks a bilingual supervisor for a cleaning company. You can call Nancy.

On the right side of the bulletin board, near the top, is a paper with the logo of some kind of Cuban agency. They are renting out space that's ideal for notaries, accountants, or financial or administrative services. They say they're in a great location, with a constant flow of customers. On the lower left corner of the agency ad is a small business card, tacked on with a round pin. It features a clown couple. The woman is wearing a white shirt with black suspenders, a red ruffled tutu, and long red-and-black socks with red combat boots. Her eyebrows are drawn over in black, with white cream makeup applied around her eyes. The man is wearing a black vest over a long-sleeved white shirt, red pants, and long socks with red-and-white shoes. His nose and cheeks are painted red. Two whole clowns. The top of the business card features their names and how to reach them if you'd like them at your party.

Dotted throughout the board are more ads from people wanting to rent out efficiency apartments, mobile homes, or a one-bedroom, one-bathroom condo.

Someone had taped a notice the size of a postcard on top of the bulletin board. Didn't bother to get the key to place it inside with the other flyers and ads. The top of the card reads HEPATIC CIRRHOSIS. On it is an illustration of a sick-looking man. His eyes are heavy and nearly closed. Next to the man is a smiling liver with rosy cheeks. A research facility is enrolling people for a study. The lower right corner reads, "Hablamos español [We speak Spanish]." But if you suspect you really have cirrhosis of the liver, maybe see your doctor first. Upon closer observation, you'll notice another copy of the study's ad is inside the bulletin board, but it had been covered by a business card promoting someone's dessert business. You'll see that sometimes—one flyer will be covered by another ad that's covered by a business card. People stay competing for space.

Just off to the right, on the bodega's brick exterior wall, is a typed ad on an 8x11 sheet of computer paper, bordered by masking tape. An adult man who doesn't smoke and doesn't drink seeks a roommate they can split rent with in the area around Gladden Park, Orlando Latin Market, and the Publix on Forty-Ninth Street. Just so you know, the man prefers a male roommate. And the writer ends the note politely, with a "gracias."

PAPI GOT JOKES

My father, Freddy, is known for his humor. Sometimes crude, sometimes corny, sometimes offensive. *I insult customers,* he told me once. *But I insult them as a joke.*

One time, my father told a man leaving the store, *Oye, no come' nada en la calle. Que están envenenando a los perros.* (Translation: Listen, don't eat anything in the street. They're poisoning dogs.)

Another time, he was talking to a customer by the register. *Oye, viejo,* he told the Nicaraguan man. *You have white hair. What's going on?*

The man joked that he had colored his hair.

Ah, me too, Freddy said, pointing to his own head that's gone beyond salt and pepper into mostly white. *I also dyed my hair white.*

Then there was the time he fused humor into a long-standing frustration. *Years ago, some customers would come in and squeeze the avocados. They'd do that to see if the avocados were ready, but they'd damage them. So one day I put a box of coconuts next to the avocados. And I put up a sign that said, "Por favor, aprieta a los cocos. No a los aguacates."* (Translation: Please squeeze the coconuts, not the avocados.)

People laughed. Sure, the sign was hilarious and cheeky. But from that point on they also treated the avocados with care.

Freddy has also left select customers with a joke disguised as unsolicited advice. He has told a few individually: *Váyase por la sombrita, porque la mierda de vaca se derrite con el sol.* (Translation: Walk in the shade, because cow dung melts in the sun.)

Another time, a man asked Papi, *Tiene higado?* (You have liver?)

My dad responded with, *Sí.* He pointed to his upper right abdomen, below his rib cage.

No, pa' vender, the man said, cracking an amused smile. He wasn't asking my father if *he* had a liver. He wanted to know if he *sold* liver in the butcher's section of the store.

Ah, sí, sí! Back there, sí! Papi responded, pointing to the carnicería a few yards away. Those of us who heard, including me, erupted in laughter.

In the summers, when el sol está que pica (see: hot, hot, hot), people stop by in search of ice. *Tienen hielo?* they usually ask. You have ice? If Papi's in a playful mood, he'll say, *Yes. Regular or dieta?* The response is usually a double glance, a quizzical look. Then laughter. A few times, customers have actually inquired further about this "diet ice" he speaks of.

One morning in June, I arrived at the bodega and saw Papi outside, loading a utility cart.

Hi, Pa, I said. *What are you doing?*

Jugando (playing). *Don't you see I'm jugando?*

I looked at the cart and saw he had on it five cases of mango nectar from Mounsier Papa. This very-dad joke was that he was *jugando*, as in jugo, as in juice, as in mango juice. How punny.

As I followed him inside, Pa struggled with the cart. He told Francisco, one of his employees, that the cart was braking. Francisco kneeled down to inspect the cart's rubber wheels. He pointed out that one of them was coming undone. Pa asked him to remove the rubber part. Francisco pulled out his boxcutter and sliced it off.

So now what? I asked Papi. *The cart's just not going to have that wheel?*

He replied, *We have to take it to the dealer now so they can replace the tires.*

Ja! Ja! Ja! (Ha! Ha! Ha!)

But Papi's not the only jokester at the bodega. Just like he playfully insults others, his employees are known to do the same back at him. Customers, too. *They call me Freddie Mercury,* he told me once. *And I tell them, "No. Freddy Krueger." Freddie Mercury, no, because he had really big front teeth. Mine are small. Freddie Mercury had his down to here. Have you seen Freddie Mercury's front teeth? Down to here.*

Many times over the years, I've watched customers laugh at his jokes, cackle at his quips. A few have told me, *Tu papá e' loco!* (Your father is crazy!)

I usually just shake my head and offer an apologetic smile before laughing along.

MESSAGES TO LA BODEGA ON FEIBU (FACEBOOK)

Does the store carry . . .

Jamaican products?

Authentic Puerto Rican pasteles?

Peruvian corn, canned or frozen?

Tortilla shaped in a bowl?

Pasteles en hoja?

Serrano ham?

Chorizo español?

Queso de freir?

Nopales frescos?

Pulled pork?

Saffron?

Homemade corn tortillas?

Fresh epazote?

Ají dulce?

Medalla Light beer?

Sofrito?

Carolina Reapers?

Jícama?

Cotija cheese?

Oregano oil?

Spanish limes?

Ropa vieja?

Mondongo?

Ginger beer?

Seven-day candles?

Cubanelle peppers?

Frozen purees?

Chorizo, estilo argentino o uruguayo?

Gazpacho?

Roasted green chiles?

Mamoncillos?

Brazilian sour tapioca starch?

A tortilla press?

Yerba mate from Argentina?

Carne de puerco?

Skirt steak?

Masa de maíz?

Colombian-style chorizo?

Quenepas?

Frozen tapas for empanadas?

Peruvian products?

Vermox?

Anything for parasite worms?

Mamey?

PAPI AT ONE OF HIS OLD BODEGAS IN BROOKLYN,
NEW YORK, SOMETIME IN THE 1990S.

BROOKLYN BODEGA BEGINNINGS

I have an old Polaroid that I stole from one of the many photo albums Mami curated of our family. Like many mothers, Damaris spent a great deal of energy taking photos of her children, developing them and arranging them neatly in sticky photo albums. Ma has stacks and stacks of albums in her house, with photos dating back to her own adolescence in both DR and New York.

As a child, I didn't particularly like posing for photos. But as an adult, I am grateful to my mother for having ignored our whining. I am glad she snapped photos of us anyway. Now I cherish these visual stamps from the past. Because, in one of these albums, I found this old Polaroid of my father inside a bodega. No date was written on the frame, but the photo was shot in the nineties. I know this because in the background of the print, tucked on a shelf atop a box of lightbulbs, is another photo of me lying on my parents' bed beside my newborn brother. I am looking up at the camera, my dark brown hair a pajón—voluminous and messy.

The bodega Papi is pictured in, I'm told, was located in Brooklyn's Flatbush neighborhood, on the corner of Newkirk and Rogers Avenues. Pa tells me he and Ma owned it at the time. In the photo my dad is a bit off-center, dressed in a pale yellow sweater with a striped navy-blue collar. A checkered graphic design is featured on its front, though I can't tell what it is exactly. Papi is young here. His dark brown hair is cut short and he sports a chevron mustache typical for that era, angled downward toward the corners of his mouth. The rest of his face is clean, though there's a hint of stubble along his jaw. He stands in what appears to be a corner of the bodega. Behind him are Chap-et lip balms, Vicks nasal inhalers, Kool-Aid packets, Bumble Bee tuna, canned sardines, and Advil. Above, displayed vertically against a white wall, is a medium-sized flag of the Dominican Republic. A visual reminder that here are dominicanos de pura cepa, as we like to say. Dominicans, from the root, through and through, are here.

By the time I was born, Papi was already a bodeguero and had been for years. He left DR for New York, like many Dominicans in the seventies and eighties, and began work at a Brooklyn bodega belonging to his Tío Bobito. The store was called Matanzas Grocery, a nod to the municipality that my grandmother and her siblings are from. After my parents got married, they bought a bodega together. My father says they named it after me. I don't remember it because I was just a baby, but I do have memories of Panchito Grocery, another Brooklyn bodega he co-owned with his eldest brother, Julio.

Over time, different communities have opened businesses in NYC that serve as a bridge between the countries they left behind and the new world they found themselves in. Irish, Italian, Jewish, and German immigrants, for example, owned grocery stores that were relied on heavily by their communities. Bodegas in particular became a pillar for Puerto Ricans as early as the 1920s, in neighborhoods like East Harlem, Williamsburg, and Red Hook. In their stores they sold plátanos, seasonings, and fruits familiar to their island. According to historian Virginia E. Sánchez Korrol, there were some two hundred Boricua bodegas or grocery stores by the late 1920s. Puerto Ricans opened not only bodegas but restaurants, botánicas, and boardinghouses. Carlos Sanabria, author of *The Bodega: A Cornerstone of Puerto Rican Barrios (The Justo Martí Collection),* said the bodega was emblematic of the need of recent arrivals for community. Much like my parents' store today, the bodega in NYC was where migrants exchanged information about jobs or apartments for rent. Over several decades, the late Cuban-born photographer Justo Martí took thousands of photos that documented the Puerto Rican and Latino community in NYC. Many featured bodegas. Sanabria said the names chosen for these stores often illustrated a clear connection to Puerto Rico. Some of the bodegas Martí captured on film had names like Vega Baja, a town in north-central Puerto Rico, Bodega Hispana Borinquen, and La Milagrosa Grocery. New York City is often referred to as a melting pot, and that is often reflected in the way the press has written about different migrant communities. In a 1959 *New York Times* article, for example, a Puerto Rican market stretching from 111th and

116th Streets on Park Avenue in East Harlem was described as the place for "unaccustomed fresh foods, such as culantro leaves, cassavas and a pumpkin-like squash called calabaza."

Dominicans, who arrived later in great numbers, also invested in bodegas. Some bought stores from aging Puerto Rican bodegueros. The Dominican bodega in NYC became a fresh take on the colmado. In DR, colmados are convenience stores often located in barrios that sell staples like milk and eggs and, similar to bodegas in the US, are spaces where neighbors gather to talk, play dominoes, or listen to music. The Dominican Republic is teeming with them. In NYC, the increasing presence of Dominican bodegas with their Spanish signs did not go over well for some who considered them outsiders. But in Santo Domingo, these workers became a symbol of progress for Dominicans everywhere. Many viewed being a bodeguero as admirable work. In NYC, ads for bodegas would begin to appear alongside other businesses in Spanish-language publications, promoting their "jugos y sodas bien fríos" (very cold juices and sodas) and "productos tropicales" (tropical products). In these newspaper ads from the 1980s, more than one store promised the freshest and cheapest products, as well as customer satisfaction. I remember Mami bringing my brother and me sometimes to visit Papi at Panchito Grocery. My memories are a kaleidoscope of visuals: My father ringing customers up. Candies packed inside Plexiglas cubbyholes. Stacks of the *New York Daily News,* which I grew up reading, by the entrance. And, of course, customers filtering in and out of the bodega with their personalities and stories.

I had a happy childhood. We lived in a two-bedroom apartment, my parents and brother and I, in a prewar building along Prospect Place. It was a very Dominican building. Just about every resident came from DR, though there were a few exceptions, like this one European viejita who lived next door to my twin best friends, Erika and Emely. And after she died, a Guyanese family moved in. But much like our building, within the walls of our apartment was a miniature Dominican Republic where Spanish was our dominant language. We watched Univision and Telemundo, ate mangú with salami y queso, and always cheered for DR in

DAMARIS AND HER DAUGHTER, AMARIS, IN THEIR APARTMENT IN CROWN HEIGHTS, BROOKLYN, SOMETIME IN THE 1990S.

the Caribbean Series. On Saturdays, nearly all apartment windows were cracked open for a collective cleaning day. From the window of our sala, I'd watch the women of our building bend this way and that, sweeping and mopping their linoleum floors, wiping dust from their appliances, all while singing loudly to a sad bolero or a delicious salsa brava.

Our mother always poured into us. She cared deeply about our education, safety, and dental hygiene. My brother and I rarely missed school, as education was the top priority. Ma always made sure we did our homework and completed our projects. So concerned was she about our education that she often drilled into me this message: She wanted us to study and get farther in our education than she and our Pa ever did. That way, we wouldn't have to endure the kind of work they've had to in this country. One time, when I was in high school, I was studying at the dining table, just yards away from my mom while she washed dishes in the kitchen. As she bent over the sink, her hands coated in suds, she delivered a whole sermon about how all she wanted was for her children to study hard. She didn't want us to toil away, exhausted, like she did. The irony was, at that very moment I legit was doing exactly what she wanted me to be doing. The message received: Get that degree so I wouldn't have to be a bodeguera like my mother.

For much of my life, Papi worked long hours to provide for us. But he still found the energy for fun. We went on family outings whenever we could. He'd take us to our many cousins' houses to play, and to Toys "R" Us to pick whatever we wanted. In the car, he'd play classics from the late Argentine singer Leo Dan. I loved our musical car rides. In DR, he'd take us to resorts and water parks, and to roadside stands in el campo for juicy mangoes. I loved to observe Papi and the way he could make just about anyone laugh. He had and still has a sense of humor that endears.

I loved my elementary school. P.S. 316 was very Black, very brown, and very Brooklyn. The front of our school had a large playground with monkey bars. We'd climb and swing, our excited squeals competing with the city buses roaring by and our hands smelling like dirty coins the rest of the day. We played clapping games like "Miss Mary Mack," "Down

Down Baby," and "Patty Cake." We jumped rope, which I loved. Double Dutch, not so much. I marveled at some of my Black friends who knew how to turn the two ropes in opposite, eggbeater-style directions. It requires coordination and a degree of fearlessness to jump in. This was back when the ropes we used were actual phone cables, so if you weren't on beat, your ankles would suffer a sting. Though Double Dutch intimidated me, I loved watching my classmates and their legs blurring to the *tsk-tsk-tsk* of the cables smacking the ground.

Being a child of Dominican immigrants in a mostly Black school meant that I was behind on some Basic Brooklyn Kid Knowledge. It was through my classmates that I learned who Lil' Kim was. On hearing I wasn't familiar with one of Brooklyn's biggest rappers of our time, they asked me, "You don't know who Lil' Kim is?!" Embarrassed, I gave a meek guess. I gestured toward a girl in our class. "Kimberly, when she was little?" You can already guess how that was received. A thunderous roar of laughter. After that, I quickly became familiar with Lil' Kim, Biggie Smalls, Jay-Z, Busta Rhymes, and most other rappers who were big at the time.

Many of us were children of immigrants. Children of the Caribbean diaspora. Haitian, Dominican, Puerto Rican, Jamaican, Trinidadian, Barbadian, Guyanese, and more. At school, we ate what they served us. At home, we ate what our parents and grandparents served us. Dominican arroz, habichuelas y carne, jerk chicken, curry goat, Haitian rice and beans, fried fish, Puerto Rican arroz con gandules, and enough plátanos to make us lethargic.

I've been taking summer trips to DR since long before I could remember them. The Dominican Republic was the only other country my parents recognized on the world map, the only other country they wanted to vacation in. There is a photo of my father and a baby me at JFK Airport, waiting for our flight to DR. So much of my love for the country comes from those summer months. DR is known for its stunning beaches, all-inclusive resorts, and music. It is also a major hub for the development of professional baseball players, with academies there that are run by all Major League Baseball teams.

But for me, the country has always been much more than that. It's where I saw myself in other Dominicans and was simultaneously reminded that I was different. Americanized. DR, to me, looks like visits to family, sitting in rocking chairs in their marquesinas, catching up over freshly squeezed lemonade or un cafecito. As a child, it looked like my mom packing an inflatable pool in her maleta, then bringing it out for us to play with our cousins on the front lawn of her childhood home in El Cibao. Looked like parties with cake in Abuela Ula's barrio to celebrate me and my younger cousin, Maria, with whom I share a birthday. Looked like going to Boca Chica, splashing in the beach's warm water and having my fill of yaniqueques, a crispy, fried dough snack. Felt like nausea when my Tío Andres drove us around endless mountains after picking us up from the airport. Sounded like a deep thirst for the English language, for any TV show in my adopted language before settling for *Friends* dubbed in Spanish. Tasted like mango, its juice dripping from my fingers to my wrist, sweetening my whole hand.

During the school year back in Brooklyn, though, I spent a lot of time indoors—playing with my brother or with my best friends, Erika and Emely, in their apartment one floor above mine. They were twins, and a year older than me, but we were sisters. I spent so much time with them that I called their parents Mamá Edna and Papi Juan. Mamá Edna would watch my brother and me regularly while my mom worked. She was truly like a bonus mom to me. The twins' grandmother, Abuela Ana, lived with them and also treated us as her own. Our parents didn't allow us to play outside without supervision, so much of our play happened indoors. We'd hide under the twins' dining table and create a world wildly different from our Prospect Place bubble. We let our imaginations run wild, believing that a fairy lived in one of Mamá Edna's dresser drawers. We were resourceful, using objects as furniture for our dolls, like the little plastic pizza savers we turned into tables for our Barbies. We embodied the Spice Girls: Emely was Baby Spice, Erika was Sporty Spice, and I was Scary Spice. We made up choreography to Britney Spears songs and imitated her vocal fry. We mourned Selena and, later, Aaliyah. We loved the Backstreet Boys and claimed three of them as our boyfriends: Erika's was Howie Dorough, Emely's was Nick Carter, and mine was Kevin Richardson. On Sundays we went to Spanish Mass at St. Teresa of Avila over on Classon Avenue. During service, we'd whisper to each other and hold in our laughter. It was a struggle to sit still, so we'd squirm in our seats until Mamá Edna reminded us that we were in a holy place. Papá Dios was watching. It was a sheltered childhood. Cautious, but happy.

But while I was being a child, my father faced trouble at work. *There were things that happened to me that I didn't want you to find out about,* Papi later told me of his time as a bodeguero in New York. *Because, ultimately as a niña, you shouldn't have to know that and suffer.*

My father had been held up at gunpoint. A few times, masked men rushed in to rob the bodega where he worked. Papi recalled being thrown down onto the floor with his coworkers. To his count, it happened five or six different times over the years. *And when that would happen, I thought only about my family. I thought about my wife and my children. Pero gracias a Dios estoy vivo* [*But thank God I'm alive*].

Papi has a rigid memory of the last bodega he had in Brooklyn. Early one morning, he went to the store to open for the day. It was winter and it had snowed. He noticed a police car parked out front. *When I went to open, the officer stepped out of the car and told me, "I'm here surveilling because the bodega was robbed last night. But we caught the robber." So the police had put on their own lock. And when I arrived, he came and unlocked it.* Papi was told there were two attempted robbers, but only one was caught. He was shown a photo of the suspect. Police asked him if he recognized the man. *I said no, that I had never seen this person.*

My father told me he later served as a trial witness. He learned that the defendant was HIV positive and needed money to buy medicine. They sentenced the man to five years. *They asked me if I needed psychological help,* Pa recalled. *But I said no—that I was fine.*

When my dad shared all this with me, I pointed out the weight of it all.

As a bodeguero in New York, you went through a lot, he said. *But what happens is, we didn't want you and your brother to know about any of that.*

FREDDY AS A YOUNG BODEGUERO
IN BROOKLYN, NEW YORK.

Pa told me my brother and I are grown now. And these events, however traumatic, happened years ago.

Crime has circled bodegas for decades. It was very visible in New York City in the 1980s and 1990s. Murders, burglaries, drug deals, theft. Bodega workers are still vulnerable to robbery, assault, and violence. And in New York City, store owners had one more worry to tack on in 2025: ATM heists. It is sadly routine to read news headlines that link bodegas to tragedy. In 1995, my Abuela Ula's cousin and his son were shot to death in their bodega in the Bedford-Stuyvesant neighborhood of Brooklyn. In 2018, a fifteen-year-old was chased by gang members and sought refuge in a Bronx bodega. It was a case of mistaken identity. Surveillance footage showed several men dragging the boy outside and stabbing him with large knives and machetes. The brutal killing sparked public outrage and calls for justice. In March 2023, a bodega worker on the Upper East Side was pistol-whipped and shot to death during a robbery. In January 2025, an on-duty letter carrier was stabbed to death inside a Harlem bodega. In August of that year, another bodega worker in East New York was fatally stabbed during a dispute over loose cigarettes. There have been many other victims of crime in bodegas. Pay attention and you'll see.

My father told me that he would, when threatened, hand money over to the perpetrators. And he developed a plan in case this were to occur again. *I would always tell the employees, "If robbers come here, tell them where the money is and don't do anything at all. Let them take the money. Because life is more valuable than money. You can always get more money, but you can't get your life back." I always told employees that.*

THE OG BODEGUERA

My father's mother, my Abuela Rosa Julia (we grandkids call her Ula), was a bodeguera at one point. I only just found out. My grandmother grew up in a rural area of Matanzas, in the Peravia Province of the Dominican Republic. She was raised with her siblings in what we call un campo. When she married my abuelo, they settled in a barrio in Santo Domingo, the capital of the Dominican Republic. In the 1950s and 1960s, many Dominicans moved from the countryside to the city. Thousands settled in informal communities on the edges of la capital. Over time, these barrios became more established.

Abuela Ula tells me she and her husband moved to their Santo Domingo barrio in 1962, the same year Papi was born. My abuelo, who was in the Dominican navy, built their first home with his hands. The house was made of wood, the floor of plain cement. *It was small,* Abuela tells me, *and we all fit there.* To better accommodate their growing family, my grandfather later built an annex, plus a kitchen. Cement blocks were eventually added to the house on Calle Sánchez. With time, it grew taller as more floors were added with new apartments that my grandmother would rent out.

Ula still lives in the same neighborhood, known as Barrio 30 de Mayo. Now in her late eighties, she is one of the OGs here. Abuela and her sister, who lives a few doors down from her, have been here since before dirt roads were passed over with gravel. The neighborhood is now crowded and busy, filled with colorful cement-block homes, apartments on top of apartments, colmados, and hair salons. It is loud, with the rumbling of motoconchos (motorcycle taxis) and the chatter of its people.

Abuela still lives in the same gated house, which has a small garage and tall iron bars out front that remain locked throughout the day. It is common in Santo Domingo to see homes and balconies enclosed in iron bars as an added layer of security. Beyond the gate door is a cozy, tile-floor porch with plastic chairs and potted plants. The house has three bedrooms, three small bathrooms, and a sala (living room) that

ABUELA ULA WAITS OUTSIDE A BODEGA.

hardly anyone sits in. Abuela's kitchen is small and smells of coffee and fruit. It has old wooden cabinets and a curtained window that looks out onto the side wall of the house next door, about a foot or two away. The backsplash, once pearl white but now ivory from age, features a hand-painted basket of vegetables.

The most lived-in space, and my favorite, is Abuela's back patio. Her terraza. There is a large fish tank to your left, a dining table, her favorite reclining chair, a TV, and a few mecedoras. Whenever I visit Abuela Ula, she is often resting in her recliner, draped in a light blanket and watching her Dominican news shows or telenovelas. Behind her is an entertainment set covered with framed photos and little owl figurines, and behind the set on the cream-colored wall are even more photos of her children, grandchildren, and great-grandchildren. The terraza is where she receives company. Whenever I visit Santo Domingo, I love to sit in one of the rocking chairs with her and look at her. I love listening to her talk and yell and carry on and sometimes complain about the loud sounds from the alley behind her home.

I love my grandmother very much. Abuela Ula is the only grandparent I have who is still alive. When I got into Columbia for graduate school, she was one of the first people I told. I asked if I could live with her while I pursued my master's degree in journalism. At the time, she still lived in Crown Heights, in the building next door to the one I grew up in. She didn't hesitate. *Claro que sí,* she told me. So began an adventure for us both. We grew closer during that year, and I'd end up staying in her apartment longer than I expected. I learned that my grandmother contains multitudes. She'd go to Mass on a Sunday, then come home and curse up a storm. When I point out her complex qualities to Ula, she just laughs and tells me that's just how she is. People are who they are.

In her house in 30 de Mayo, Abuela's only pets are her fish. But there are the street cats. They slink through the back iron bars, walk across her terraza, through her house, and onto Calle Sánchez out front. And she lets them.

When we moved to my house, where I still live, my husband and I started a bodeguita, Abuela tells me one day. *Of course it wasn't—*

De verdad? I interrupt. *For real?*

Abuela Ula insists it wasn't a big bodega. *It was a bodeguita chiquita, and my husband would tend to it. And when he had to step out, I would take over. But I didn't like it. I don't like being stuck in a bodega.*

I want to know more. When I ask Ula why she didn't really like working in her bodega, she can't really answer. Just laughs. Says she preferred cooking for her children. But I press her: *But what is it that you didn't like about being in the bodega? Being behind the register?*

Well, she begins, *because it was a bodega chiquita, in a barrio that was not yet populated. One customer would come in, and the next one wouldn't arrive until an hour later. You spent the whole day there . . .*

She sucks her teeth. She can still taste the decades-old memory.

At my grandparents' bodeguita, they sold rice, beans, cooking oil, beer, rum, cigarettes—everything Abuela Ula says you would find in a Dominican colmado today. It was her husband's idea to open a bodega. *But I don't know what for, because he was in the Dominican navy. He was also a cabinetmaker and a carpenter. Customers would ask him to make a bedroom set, a dining set. He could do everything customers asked for.* My abuela felt there was no need to also open a store. *I didn't think so,* she says, *because that's a kind of esclavitud.* I have heard that before. Some bodegueros say the bodega life is a form of slavery because of the unforgiving hours and heavy workload. This is not a fair comparison at all, but language can sometimes fail us. Perhaps what my grandmother felt was trapped.

Abuela later became an entrepreneur. She'd travel to Puerto Rico to buy clothes, then come back and sell them right in her home. *Las vecinas would stop by to browse, and they'd buy.*

So it was like a clothing store in your house? I ask. Abuela says it was, but she didn't have the clothes shelved or anything like that. She would bring the merchandise in a maleta, and the neighbors would come by and check them out. *And they would pull the clothes from the maleta, look*

ABUELA ULA IN ORLANDO LATIN MARKET.

at them, and decide if they wanted to purchase them, I say. *Exactly,* she confirms. I tell Abuela that she's a matatana, which, in Dominican, means she is a boss bitch. She laughs.

I always wish my grandfather was still alive. Papi tells me he died at home, in his sleep. Pa, the baby of the family, was about ten years old. I tell Abuela, *Que pena that I could never meet Abuelo.*

Ay, sí, she says. After decades, my abuela's voice is still sad when she speaks of her late husband. My heart aches for her. *He was so good. He was a good, good man. We were married seventeen years when he died. We had only seventeen years.*

I tell her how sorry I am. She thanks me and tells me that's how it is. That's life. My abuela lost her love. She became a widow overnight, with four children to raise. I want her to know that I also loved him, even if I never met him. I share with Abuela, *Papi tells me that he was a good dad, and that he would have been a very good grandfather.* She cries out. *Ay! He loved children! The children from the barrio would run to him. He would carry them with one hand, like this.* She lifts her left arm, palm open. *Pues, sí. Era bueno, bueno.* [*Well, yes. He was good, good.*]

At home, they were a team. My grandfather would pull his weight around the house. I imagined that was rare in those times. Abuela confirms so. *Ay, sí. That was very rare. There was a lot of machismo,* she says. *He would mop the floors and would prepare the raw meat and fish for our meals, because he was raised in a house that had a fish and butcher shop.* Ula says he was raised differently.

I already know, but I ask my abuela if she had a good love for seventeen years. She nods and tells me she did. I tell her that I'm happy she had that in her life, and that my grandfather had her. I feel for Ula, who never remarried after her husband died. *Thank you for talking with me,* I say. *I love speaking with you.* We hug, and I can still feel her grief. I wish I could extract it from her, but it is immovable. I tell her I love her.

DOWN THE AISLE

previous AISLE 4 OF ORLANDO LATIN MARKET, WHERE YOU CAN FIND CRACKERS, FLAVORED WAFERS, BARS OF CHOCOLATE, AND CANS OF CONDENSED MILK.

CAN THEY BE A WITNESS?

Hermenegildo comes into the store one April day like he usually does—with an aura of calm about him. He is dressed in a striped BOSS shirt, light khaki slacks, and a cream-colored cap with "NY" on it. From the stack near the register, the retired shoemaker selects a red basket and begins making his way around the store. Among the items on his shopping list are yogurt, tamales, and milk. "Sometimes I arrive here and I come for one thing," he explains, "but then I see something else that interests me." Hermenegildo is a longtime customer. He has been buying food from Orlando Latin Market since before my parents took over the business. "Truthfully, I feel good about the service here. I feel at home." If he didn't, you would not see him here. *Trust.*

Hermenegildo is from Pinar del Río, on the far western end of Cuba, but has lived in St. Petersburg with his wife, Vitalia, for years. I politely ask him for his age.

"Yo tengo ochenta y ocho años," he answers.

"And how do you feel at your age?" I ask.

"How do I feel at my age?" he asks in turn. "The same way you feel at your age."

His Cuban Spanish is so fast that I have to confirm what he just said.

"The same, what?"

"The same way you feel at your age."

I understand what he's trying to say. He is letting me know: *He's eighty-eight. And? Why wouldn't he feel good at his age?*

"Bien," I reply, humbled but fine with it. Hermenegildo then places his basket down in the middle of the aisle. I watch him, wondering what he's about to do. He bends his knees and begins doing squats.

One, two, three.

OK, we are doing this.

"Cuatro, cinco," I say, amused.

Six, seven.

"No, I can do more," he insists.

My lesson: *Hermenegildo is not one to play with. He will let you know.*

I tell him I believe him. That I couldn't do all that. "So you're very active," I say.

He then restarts the squats, instructs me to count.

Uno, dos, tres, cuatro, cinco . . .

We count together in Spanish. My Tía Margarita, who is behind the register, sees us in the aisle. She laughs at the scene unfolding before her. She encourages Hermenegildo, who continues bending his knees down to the speckled floor. He doesn't stop until he hits thirty. "Wow!" I extend a high-five to him. Hermenegildo insists again that he can do more. And again, I insist that I believe him. He laughs.

It's a moment of playfulness for a man who usually carries a more serious demeanor. Hermenegildo is a devout Jehovah's Witness. Decades ago, he was one of many Cubans against Fidel Castro's regime. In the face of dissent, the revolutionary government punished, ostracized, and jailed nonconformists. Hermenegildo tells me he was thrown in jail several times, unjustly. During one such stint, Hermenegildo, twenty-six at the time, met a Jehovah's Witness who told him about another government called the Kingdom of God. Witnesses believe there is a real government in heaven that will replace human-led governments. Hermenegildo felt a shift that day and soon became a Witness himself. Now it's his faith that makes him happy, fulfilled.

"You don't decide to become a Jehovah's Witness," he tells me. "God chooses you." To Hermenegildo, faith means life, and the author of life is God. "He's given me instructions on how to extend my lifespan," he says, his tone serious. "And life extends with the steps you take." He cautions about mujeriegos (womanizers) and diseases that lead to malnutrition. He has hope for a different government. "A different world where you and I won't die and won't grow old. God says he doesn't want his children to grow old."

Hermenegildo encourages young people to study the Bible. He believes doing so will keep them healthy. "Why? Because then you avoid drugs, drunkenness," he explains. "You avoid being a mujeriego. A man can have a woman, but one." He raises his index finger. "One woman."

After reading and learning the Bible, you begin teaching it. That's how Hermenegildo sees it. He tells me that he's teaching me the Bible without me realizing it. Jesus, Hermenegildo adds, testified about his Father. "Like you would like to share the good examples of your father. Isn't that true?" he asks. "Because you're not going to share the bad things about your papá, if you know something. You share the good things."

I listen.

"That's what God wants, that both you and I share good things about him," Hermenegildo continues on. "Because we're his children. The breath you receive—"

He pauses. Inhales deeply.

"Is from him."

—

After I spoke with Hermenegildo, his wife Vitalia began calling me. At 9 a.m. on Fridays, I'd see her number pop up on my cell phone screen. She wanted to speak with me about God. Wanted to know about my purpose. During one of our calls, I had what some may call an epiphany. Would Vitalia be interested in sharing her Word with me? Yes, of course she would. Which is how I found myself seated in her tidy dining room, on my lunch break one Wednesday afternoon in June. *My parents came to know the truth of the Bible in 1943,* she told me. *I was a little girl, only dos añitos. I was born in 1941. But I learned what they had been learning. And that's how we began sharing testimonies about what the Bible teaches.*

Vitalia was baptized as a Jehovah's Witness at twelve. And since then, she's tried to offer free biblical courses to people. She wants them to know about the Word of God. *In reality most people need a life change, but an earthly, human change. Understand? That's what the Bible shows. Dios—Jehová Dios, which is the true name of God—his name means "él hace que llegue a ser" ("he causes to become"). That's to say he has a purpose for humankind. And this purpose is described in the Bible from the very beginning of humankind, in the book of Genesis.*

She went on to tell me the story of Adán y Eva—Adam and Eve.

According to the Bible, she said, God created the first humans in a garden. The Garden of Eden. She told me of the instructions handed down to them, that they could eat from all the trees in the garden, except one. *It was like when parents tell their children, "Don't touch that because it can cause you harm." Verdad? That's what God did with the first couple. It was a test of obedience.*

We all know what happened. They didn't pass. *But even with the failure of the obedience test, Jehová Dios didn't think all was lost. No,* Vitalia told me. *He made a promise that he would have a son who, with time, would crush the head of the enemy. So the humankind that came from Adán y Eva could have a new perspective. An offspring. Do you know who that descendencia was? Jesús Cristo. Jesús Cristo was that descendencia that God had promised.*

Vitalia insisted that we are all imperfect sinners. That this is why we get sick, grow old, and pass away. She spoke to me about Jesus. *Jesús Cristo lived on Earth for thirty-three and a half years, preached the purpose of God and the hope to be perfect. That's the purpose of God.* She said humanity is in such a deplorable state, which I don't entirely disagree with.

I am secure because I know the biblical story, she said with conviction. *God does not lie. And this was left for us, written, so we can know how humankind began, what happened in the beginning, and why we have this condition of sin and death. And if God is perfect and eternal, why do we as his children have to die? I know this story because it's not just a story. It's reality.*

ILEANA'S MAMI

Those childhood grocery trips remain vivid in Ileana's mind. She and her mother, Miriam, would step out of their Los Angeles home and walk to one of their favorite markets. Miriam couldn't drive, nor did she care to learn, so she and her only child would often walk to an Argentine-owned grocery store they called La Catalina. There was also Villalobos Market, which Ileana remembers was Mexican-owned. Even back then, Ileana recognized these stops as an errand. They were journeys, albeit short, but they were journeys they underwent together. "It'd be a chore, so to speak, right? But it always felt nice, because I'm with her," Ileana says. "I'm seeing her in her element, getting all her ingredients, making all of her lists." There were always to-do lists crafted by Miriam in their studio apartment. Born in El Salvador, Miriam was very organized, very type A. As a mother and wife, she kept lists of the chores she needed to do at home. As a housekeeper, she kept track of how much clients paid her, which houses she would be going to on which days, and if a family would be out of town on a certain week.

Miriam kept a pocket-sized notebook with her at all times for jotting down what they needed. Young Ileana would look up at her mother, watch her contemplate which was the right vegetable or fruit to get. Watch her calculate if one was not *too* ripe, if another would soon go bad. She'd watch her mami think it over, deciding whether she would cook something that night or the following day. "Making all of those strategic decisions that a lot of mothers, in particular, make when they're thinking about the meals that they're going to be cooking."

Her childhood years inched forward, and mother and daughter went on many more short journeys for groceries. The year Ileana would turn fifteen, the family of three received devastating news. Miriam had cancer. The diagnosis hit them at the very beginning of the year, in January. Miriam began treatment and fought hard. Months went by. She fought harder. The family continued planning for Ileana's quinceañera, to be held in late July. "She was very terrified of not making it to my quinceañera," Ileana remembers.

Throughout her childhood on Ileana's birthday, her mother would always enter her room in the middle of the night, which was around the time she was born. She'd go to Ileana's bedside and plant a happy birthday kiss on her forehead. "For the fifteenth birthday, I do remember her once again kissing me awake. But kissing me awake with tears, because she was terrified that she wasn't going to make it to see me turn fifteen." The quince still went on as scheduled, and Miriam was able to attend. They kept it small because they didn't want her exposed to big crowds. The family tried to keep her as safe as possible.

But cancer doesn't care that you have a daughter, or a husband, or a full life. Cancer doesn't give a damn about the dreams you have for your family, or the to-do lists you put so much thought into. Miriam's cancer was quick. It was aggressive. As cancer cells spread throughout her body, she continued the battle. She spent more and more time in the hospital.

But in the end, cancer took the beloved wife and mother away. Miriam died in November, at age fifty-six.

Losing one's mother is a profound and enduring grief. Losing your mother just after turning fifteen is deeply unfair. "She was supposed to teach me how to do my makeup once I turned fifteen," Ileana says. "I lost out on a lot of conversations that we were supposed to have once I was 'a young woman of society,' having turned fifteen."

The years stretched on, and Ileana grew into adulthood with a lasting absence. She graduated and became a journalist and a writer. Years ago, when she moved to St. Pete, a friend told her about Orlando Latin Market. "I came here, and I felt like I was transported back to my childhood of shopping at La Catalina and Villalobos," Ileana says. "The smells that you get because there's a counter with fresh-made food, all of the sourced ingredients from all over Latin America." Together we step out of the storage room and enter aisle after aisle, searching for products from her childhood. Here, Ileana finds the kind of vanilla wafers her mother used to buy her, the rectangular ones with a grid pattern. In another aisle she finds Knorr's chicken flavor bouillon in a box. She says she opts for the jar. "I use it in rice 'cause that's what my mom would do, to give the rice a little bit of a kick," she says. "We would use jasmine rice with Knorr."

Miriam left her daughter many lessons. She taught Ileana about responsibility and accountability. "If you're a host, if you are having someone enter your home, there's a responsibility and a mutual sign of respect of making them feel as comfortable as possible," Ileana says. "Likewise, whenever we would go to other people's homes, she would tell me, *You have to be a respectful guest as well. Somebody is letting you into their personal space. Somebody is making you feel comfortable with food, with conversation, with telenovelas—if people are coming over to watch the finale.*" Ileana's mami taught her about respect, about offering to assist in tidying up after gatherings, all these teachings that have stayed with Ileana. She instilled Salvadoran culture in Ileana. She also raised her to be bilingual. A gift.

Ileana has now been living longer without her mother than she did with her. But she continues carrying out her mami's teachings. She also inherited the same affinity for making to-do lists. "My mom was a very special person," Ileana says. "I miss her every day."

AN INTIMATE SANCOCHO

Negrito stops by Orlando Latin Market on a late Sunday morning in early November. He's here to do his part in the making of a sancocho. He needs white rice, guineos, and plátanos—must-haves for the meat and vegetable stew. "I come here every day," the eighty-seven-year-old says in Dominican singsong. He stands in front of the open-air cooler. He has already selected a bunch of guineos and set them aside, and now he digs for the best available green plantains. The cardboard box lined with plastic is filled with them. Some are thinner than others, but all are the same bright green, and two for a dollar. What Negrito looks for in a plátano is simple. He checks out their size. He prefers the bigger ones because, the thicker they are, the more light-yellow flesh to boil or dice and fry. Negrito picks and picks until he has five plantains. He sets those aside, too. He lifts his chin up toward the upper shelves of the open-air cooler. His eyes are behind rectangular-shaped glasses, shaded by a Tampa Bay Rays hat. Negrito reaches up and picks up two more guineos. He studies the unripe bananas before tossing them back onto the shelf. Picks up a bigger bunch and studies it as well. His sister-in-law is going to make the sancocho, and he will help. They have all they need except for the few items he has to pick up today.

He was born José but, in Spanish, family and friends call him Negro or Negrito. A term of endearment for Dominicans. Negrito has a large extended family in St. Pete. And every Friday, they gather. Multiple generations under one roof, theirs is a weekly interweaving of conversations and laughter over food, drink, and music. But the sancocho being planned on this Sunday is not like those gatherings. This one is for himself, his wife, and his sister-in-law. Small and intimate.

Sancocho is a cherished dish in the Dominican Republic. There are sancochos from other countries, too. Puerto Rico, Trinidad and Tobago, Colombia, Honduras, Cuba, Mexico, to name a few. And it has different names depending on where you're from. Sancoche, sopa de res, ajiaco. There are variations of sancocho even in DR and across the

Dominican diaspora. It is a laborious, multistep process that involves seasoning and cooking the meat, adding water to a large pot, and then dropping in chopped plátanos and root vegetables like yuca and yautía. The recipe calls for all this while remembering to add ingredients from the longest-cooking ones to the shortest-cooking ones, in that order.

Negrito tells me he does not take the lead in making the sancocho, but he assists his cuñada. "I go and fetch the materials and everything," he says, "because my wife isn't doing very well." He also peels the plátanos to prepare them for boiling. Negrito says he loves his sancocho with arroz blanco. White rice is a frequent companion to the stew, along with slices of avocado.

Later, Negrito stands at the end of the aisle where the root vegetables are piled in cardboard boxes. He rests his left hand on one of the green-painted wooden shelves, peers up and down at the rows of víveres while he thinks. He's running through the list in his mind.

Finally, he steps away.

"We have guineo, we have batata, we have plátanos," he says loudly to himself. "Let's go pay."

Our bodega tour begins shortly after noon on a Tuesday in March. We're standing in the very back of the store. The air around aisle 5 is a dizzying smell of bleach and cleanliness. My friend Gloria and I pause before the shelves of dish soap and small bags of detergent powder. "Let's start with the candles," Gloria says. "Velas." She gestures with her left hand toward one of the middle shelves, a small section of which has rows of short candles in blue, yellow, red, and white. Nearby are candles of saints for worshippers to pray over. Gloria's right hand holds a small Malta bottle, which she has been savoring since she arrived. "Very important," she says of the velas. "Love them."

A few items down, Gloria points to a row of familiar cylinder tubes. "Comet is like my home's cleaning section growing up." She cups her hand over the containers of Ajax cleaner next to the Comet brand. "Ajax," Gloria says, pronouncing it in Spanish—where the *j* sounds like the letter *h*. "Or Ajax," she adds, pronouncing it like Americans do.

"We call it Aha!" I interject, referring to how my Dominican mom says it.

"Aha," she says.

We laugh.

Gloria then turns her attention to Fabuloso. The liquid cleaners shine pretty colors in their bottles. Like jewels—purple, red, and green. "Fabuloso.com all day, every day," she says.

"What about Mistolín?" I ask my friend. "Did you ever use Mistolín?" The bottles of my favorite floor cleaner are located one shelf below Fabuloso. Gloria tells me she hadn't. I rave about the lilac Mistolín. It's what my mother often used. And now I use it at home. But for Gloria it was purple Fabuloso all the way.

When we reach the end of the aisle, we make a sharp left and step into the sweets aisle.

"Ah, hot chocolate!" Gloria gushes. She pats a resealable package of a long block of Corona cocoa. This traditional Colombian hot chocolate is infused with cloves and cinnamon. "The real. The bar." Gloria points to another hot chocolate package. "This is the best one," she tells me. It is yellow and green, also from the Corona brand. The front of the package features an image of a green mug of hot chocolate.

"So this is the one that Colombians like?" I ask.

"Yeah," she confirms. "I haven't had the cloves and cinnamon. I bet it's good. I have the traditional."

—

Gloria's Colombian parents live near my parents' bodega and shop here sometimes. They've come here for hot food, for yuca chips, for Malta. I didn't know this when Gloria and I became friends a few years ago.

I lead Gloria to the bodega's very back corner, where the storage room is. It would be a boring room with worn white walls were it not for its busyness. There are shelves lined with disposable containers and cups, sacks of dry beans, and boxes and boxes of merchandise destined for the store floor. Gloria's eyes light up from behind her big round glasses when she sees the tall stacks of Malta India, bottles and bottles of it wrapped in plastic. She pulls out her phone and snaps a photo.

"It's my favorite Malta. It's the best," she says. "I love seeing it all stacked up here."

Growing up in a Colombian household, Malta India was a treat because you couldn't find the best brands just anywhere. "But the good brands, you can only find at bodegas or at Colombian bakeries—panaderías—where you go in, you get your bread, you get your Malta and it's like, *Ahh, you're set.*" She understands that Malta is not soda, technically. It's a malted beverage. As a child, Gloria always wanted to drink coffee, but she wasn't allowed to. While it's normal for her family to drink it today from sunrise to sunset, she says she was only permitted to try coffee when she was about fourteen. But she could drink Malta. And though Malta is not coffee, one can argue it looks like it. "So when I was younger, drinking Malta always felt like a little rebellion," she says with a mischievous smile. "I could have this special treat, this special drink that looked like coffee. It's just a delight. It also reminds me of these spaces—of bodegas and of panaderías and of Colombian restaurants."

A poet and author, Gloria was born and raised in St. Pete. Like many others who lead diasporic lives, she describes herself as Colombian American. "I think Colombian first, on purpose," she says, "because it's the thing about me that could be erased, I think, by somebody looking at me." Today Gloria wears her short brown hair down, curled out at the bottom. She has on black pants and a brown sweater with thin black stripes. From her neck hangs a chain with three pendants. The first is a round pendant of a crescent moon. Earth's only natural satellite is a relief accompanied by three stars. "The number three has come up a lot," she explains, "and I saw this and was like, *That's mine.*" The second pendant, made of brass, is a hand, face down. From it sprouts a flower. "I love this one, because I'm always thinking of my hands like a writer and like a creative person. Like somebody who wants to use my hands to make art and make things that make a difference in the world." The third pendant is a mal de ojo. Half of its blue iris is faded around a black pupil. It's meant to protect against the evil eye. Colombians, Gloria says, are very superstitious. She bought this one at a mall in Bogotá and has worn it since she was fourteen years old. That's around the age when Gloria began working.

One summer while working at Bath & Body Works, a teenaged Gloria found herself covered in these smells that she could no longer tolerate. Then came a breakthrough. She realized that, from that point on, she only wanted to work in creative jobs. So she did. She became deeply involved in the arts. As an adult, Gloria's own works as a writer and poet are conceived and developed through a Colombian American lens. She was raised in a house where her parents spoke Spanish first. Her family learned English together. The *Colombian* in *Colombian American* is very much part of her identity, she contends. In how she perceives the world. The *Colombian* half is never secondary, which she points out is why she likes to lead with that. "And because it's the thing that I know, now as a mom, can be erased," she says. "It can be lost, or can be diluted. And I think the world, especially right now at every turn, is trying to do that. It's trying to erase people's culture and individuality and push us all towards one North Pole that looks very similar."

And what of the *American* part of *Colombian American?* "I love this place. It's somewhere that's hard to love sometimes, as we know," she says, her voice sincere. "I love this sense of opportunity, for lack of a better word, that is here. And that so many people are here because they have need and desire." The way Gloria sees it, the United States has reinvented itself repeatedly. She believes it to be inspiring as a setting. For her, America looks like a place that's welcoming and diverse. "I love a country that can reinvent itself and that can inspire people to really dream, and I try to hold onto *that.*"

Once we are done gushing over traditional Colombian hot chocolate, Gloria continues moving slowly down the sweets aisle. "I love Lecheritas." Her voice bubbles into a laugh. We both look toward the middle shelf, where there are stacks of La Lecherita sweetened condensed milk. The small cans are billed as a perfect snackable size. Gloria picks one up. "When we were little, my dad would open a hole in the top of these," she says, bringing the can up toward her face. "And we would put it in the fridge and we'd just take a sip." Gloria makes a motion with her hand as if she's really drinking some. They'd take sips of La Lecherita throughout the week. "So healthy," she says sarcastically. "But I love this condensed milk."

We reach the end of the aisle of sweets and turn right. Aisle 3 is lined with sacks of flour, raisins, and bricks of panela. "This is what I'm talking about," Gloria muses aloud. She reaches up to a shelf on our left and picks up a tall glass jar of coffee. The label reads Colcafé. It's a popular brand of Colombian instant coffee. In the center of the label is a glass cup of steaming black coffee, with three coffee beans clustered near the bottom. "Intense bold instant coffee," she points out, is what her family drinks. She looks around and notices the Italian-style Vigo breadcrumbs. "That's how my mom got me to eat meat," she shares. "I don't eat meat now, but that was the way she convinced me, was covering it in breadcrumbs." Two shelves up are boxes with rectangular packets of atole from the Klass brand. The traditional drink is made from masa. They come in different flavors. "I loved this stuff when I was sick," Gloria shows me, pointing to a vanilla packet. "Did you have this when you were sick? Like Maizena?"

"Oh, yeah! I did," I say. "It'd be warm. It'd be hot."

"Like cornstarch," Gloria says, pointing next to the bright yellow boxes of Maizena. "The strawberry one is good." Waving her right hand over the whole shelf, she tells me this was her "sick food." Not Jell-O, she clarifies, but products like Maizena and the packets of atole.

She takes a few steps until we reach another area of the shelf. We could call this "Little Colombia." "Here we go, pandebono," she announces. "This is my section. This is my favorite food." The box is white, with the word *Pandebono* up top in bold red type. It features the three horizontal bands of the Colombian flag: yellow, blue, and red. There's also a photo of a bunch of pandebonos, a type of Colombian bread made of cassava starch, cheese, and eggs. Pandebonos usually come in a ring shape, which is how they are pictured on the box. "These are so hard to make," Gloria says exasperatingly. "Exceedingly hard to make. It's so wild." She has tried to make pandebonos, but it's a delicate process. Sometimes they come out amazing, she says. Other times, not so much.

Nearly two months ago, Gloria celebrated the publication of her debut YA novel, *This Is the Year.* The book follows Julieta Villarreal, a teen who lives under a crushing weight rooted in desperation about the state of Florida and the world. She's also in a deep grief, having lost her twin sister, Ofelia, in a hit-and-run. Julieta, like Gloria, is Colombian American. My friend recalls drafting the book during a very strange time. "It was written during the pandemic, and I was looking at Florida and thinking about the future of this place. And again, that idea of reinvention and change and evolution that I think we're resistant to sometimes. It's very necessary and, if we don't step into it, the environment will make us step into it."

Gloria loves Florida and how strange and beautiful it is. She loves its people. She thinks its diversity is incredible. She believes there's so much good community here, and that there are people doing the work at every level, in all kinds of places. Yet the relationship between her and Florida is complicated. "I have also been shown what this state is again and again, by the people who are running it," she says somberly. "And that's something I can't ignore."

She thinks about this often as a parent and as a woman. She wants to think Florida is changing for the better. But she's been hoping for a long time. "I'm in a tricky place with the state. It'll always be home, but I don't know if physically I will always live here."

MIGUEL IN AISLE 1
AT ORLANDO LATIN MARKET.

MIGUEL MOVES ON

Miguel stands in front of packaged noodles, rice, and cooking oils. Aisle 2 is where you'll find bagged dry beans—lentils, guandules/gandules/pigeon peas, white and gold hominy. There are rows of salad olives, Manzanilla olives, olives for your cocktail, liquid sazón, jars of yellow hot peppers, and ají panca. On this late Sunday morning in early March, Miguel is on FaceTime with his cousin. He holds his cell phone in his left hand and a forty-ounce bottle of Mazola corn oil in his right. "Ya?" he asks his cousin, a small face on his screen. He wants to know if that is the size she wants. It isn't. "That's the biggest bottle," Miguel points out in Cuban Spanish, placing it back on the shelf. He then turns to me. "Mi vida, do you have a bigger bottle than this?" He picks it up again to show me. "I don't know if you work here."

"Déjame ver," I say. "No, I don't work here." Not anymore. But I turn to look for my mom who is at the register. "Mami, is there a bottle bigger than this?" I ask her. "Mazola?" She tells me they have it in a gallon. The customer, hearing my mother, turns back to his cousin on the phone. "Do you want it in a gallon, then, Monica? That's what she told me. They have the big gallon." Miguel tells me that he's shopping for his prima. He jokes that she likes to stay home and do nothing, hence why he is here now, doing the grocery shopping for her.

Together we return to aisle 2. I point to where the gallons of Mazola oil are on a bottom shelf. Miguel stoops down and selects one. Each bottle features the popular brand name in green gradient, and behind it an ear of corn. "Is this the one, Monica?" he asks again. He lifts the yellow gallon next to his bespectacled face.

"Sí," she says.

"Perfecto."

Miguel feels sluggish this morning. "This is early for me," he says. On weekends, he usually sleeps in. But this particular Sunday is different. He is here at Orlando Latin Market for one main reason. "I broke my cousin's mop," he says sheepishly, a small laugh slipping from his mouth.

"And she told me to go get her a new one here, because this is where she gets them at." The floor squeegee he came for is what Cubans call a haragán. Miguel drove forty minutes from Clearwater to St. Pete to get one. The replacement, a shiny blue pole, was one of the first things he placed in the shopping cart before tackling a bigger grocery list. Miguel, tall and slender, wears a black collared shirt, brown plaid pajama pants, and some winter shoes he bought recently for a trip to Gatlinburg, Tennessee. His brown hair is tousled, framing a handsome face with a nose ring. From his neck hangs a cross made of green stone that belonged to his abuela. Miguel says she had bought it in Italy decades ago. Her birthstone was peridot, his is emerald, and so he found a way to melt the stones together. She died a year ago.

Miguel's shoes shuffle against the floor as he returns to his cart parked next to an ice cream freezer. He nestles the gallon of corn oil next to a big sack of rice. In the cart's baby seat are packs of Petit apple and mango nectars. In the main basket are a six-pack of Malta Hatuey, soda crackers, and Café La Llave. "What else?" he asks. His cousin informs him that malanga and calabaza are next on the list. He begins walking toward the back of the store. "That should be around here," he mutters to himself. I tell him "Over here," leading the way down aisle 4. We pass cans of coconut milk, Inca Kola, and wafers in dulce de leche, vanilla, guava, chocolate, coconut, and pineapple flavors. Above us, on the top shelf, are tubs of soda crackers and Florecitas with their crisp, round bottoms and dollops of white and pastel-colored icing on top.

Miguel speaks like a native Cuban because he is one. He's from Bauta, a city in west-central Cuba that's considered part of the Havana metropolitan area. He was eleven when he moved to the United States. As he grew from an adolescent to a young adult, Miguel learned the art of code-switching, of shifting between languages, vocabularies, and behaviors. He says how he is around white people is different from how he is around other Cubans. "When I'm around my people, I act like I don't know English," he laughs. Miguel is twenty-one now. At this point, he's lived here almost as long as he lived in his island country. "I feel like I'm in Cuba," Miguel notes as he observes all the merchandise around him. Then, as quickly as the words come out, he takes them back. "Well, never mind. I do not feel like I'm in Cuba 'cause when I go to Cuba, all these shelves are empty." Here, though, Miguel finds products that tug at his memory. He spots Malta Bucanero, a nonalcoholic malt beverage that's considered a Cuban staple. He sees yuca and plátanos. Still, he admits to feeling a bit lost when he arrives at the bodega. He says he doesn't usually get his groceries at Latin grocery stores. His cousin gave him a list of common items, but it wasn't specific enough for Miguel. No brands were listed, so the best thing for him to do was to get her on the phone.

We are now in front of the víveres. Miguel pulls a clear produce bag from its vertical holder. "How many malangas do you want?" he asks his prima. He rests his phone on a circular flat piece of metal, the top of the bag holder. She wants five. "Five malangas?" Miguel wants to confirm. His fingers work the top end of the bag to open it. Affirmative. She wants five.

From a cardboard box Miguel picks up a long piece of malanga that loosely resembles a knobby tree branch. Above the boxes, on a large slab of wood that's part of the overall display, is a sign in Spanish that reads: *Por favor no partir las malangas.* Translation: *Please don't break the malangas.* Another sign in all caps more bluntly reads: *Sea educado. No partir las viandas.* Translation: *Be educated. Don't break the root vegetables.* Some customers will take a yuca or malanga and slam it against the corner of the box to break a piece off. They do this because they want to ensure the inside is still good. Not rotten. "Are these the malangas?" Miguel asks me. Yes, I say, but point out there are different kinds. Directly in front of us are malanga isleña and malanga lila. His cousin, still on the phone, tells him she wants la malanga blanca. Miguel places five in the bag and clutches the top closed with his fist.

Next up is the cut calabaza. I lead Miguel and his cousin on the phone to the row of fridge doors that take up nearly the whole back wall of the store. Miguel now stands in front of the door to the far left. He holds his phone up, away from his face, so his cousin can see the large chunks of calabaza wrapped in cellophane on the screen.

"These?" he asks.

Yes, those.

"How many?"

Her voice is choppy, so he brings the phone to his right ear.

"How many?" he asks again.

Once Monica tells him, Miguel places the phone on a case of water behind him. He shakes another clear produce bag until it opens up. His hands reach inside the box and he picks two pieces of calabaza. He drops them in. "Can I get picadillo to make pasta today?" Miguel asks his cousin. "And salsa Ragú?" He carries the clear bags filled with chunks of calabaza and malanga blanca down the aisle, makes a sharp right, and passes through the sweets aisle again. "Avocado, culantro, and cilantro," Miguel rattles off. He places the bags in the small cart, by now nearly overflowing.

This grocery run, like countless others, is mostly uneventful. Errands are an immovable, routine part of life. Groceries need to be bought. We all need to eat. But elsewhere in Miguel's world, there is a big moment on the horizon. He's been attending trucking school. The following week, he is set to graduate and earn his trucker license. "I'm gonna be trucking with my partner—because he's already a truck driver—for like months and making money so we can pay for his school, my school, and then just not have to struggle anymore." Miguel says he once spent a year living in his car. To make money, he would offer to drive people long distances. "I would tell people, *Hey, if you need to go from here to Canada, I'll drive you. Just give me like nine hundred dollars and I got you. If you need to move all your stuff in my car, I'll move all your stuff in my car*," he recalls. "So that's pretty much what I was doing." He realized then how much he loves driving. *This is the shit,* he thought. He loves cruising by and watching the world around him. "I can open my window, I can listen to music," he gushes. He tilts his head up, daydream-like. "Sometimes I open my window, and I like people looking at me. I want the spotlight on me. I like singing and being loud, so they can look at me." He laughs. In the car, Miguel jams to soft R&B and R&B fused with rock. He enjoys Latin music sometimes, but his taste is very specific. "I don't like reggaeton," he says flatly. "I know that's probably a crime in the Hispanic community, but I don't like reggaeton." To him, reggaeton is less danceable. His family, he adds, is also pretty religious. "I know it's a little bit hypocritical 'cause I'm gay, but still, me and my partner go to church every Sunday and we're more than welcomed. I don't like a lot of music that says a lot of curse words, or where it's very dirty, because I can't listen to it in front of my family."

Once Miguel and his partner hit the road, they plan to blast the music they love. And they'll bring along their pets: a newly adopted merle dachshund named Armani, a black cat named Chanel, and an orange tabby cat named Tipsy.

There was also a time not long ago when Miguel pursued another dream. "I was gonna be an actor," he tells me. He rubs his fingers together. "But no dinero." This dream led Miguel down to Miami and to Los Angeles for casting calls. But his efforts to become a working actor were unsuccessful. "It was too expensive to buy my way into it, and there was a lot of people buying their way into it. And I wasn't gonna compete with that. So I just kind of like . . . I didn't give up, but I gotta move on. I can't get stuck in that."

Miguel refocuses his attention on the shopping list, abandoning the cart again. We pass the voice of Marc Anthony playing on Mami's Bluetooth. The salsero sings of a former lover in denial about her feelings for him. Soon Miguel and I are standing in front of the open-air cooler containing red and green peppers, guineos verdes (green bananas), five-piece bags of garlic, and more. He holds onto the phone with his right hand, scratches his back with his left. He's thinking. He scans the cooler and turns around. That's when Miguel spots them. "Here they are," he says. Next to a box of pineapples are the aguacates. Big round avocados. He places two in a bag, then goes over to pick a box of sazón by the root vegetables. "Mi vida, where did you tell me the culantro and cilantro are?" he asks me. I point him to the area where he had just been. The bunches of culantro and cilantro are kept together in a hollow metal bin filled with water. "La bolsita," I say as I reach up near the top of the cooler and yank a bag from the holder. I hand it to him.

"Ay, Monica," he whines softly to his cousin who is still on the phone. "You have me as if we had gone to Walmart." She says she's sorry, apologetically yet firm. "You're already there," she adds.

Miguel returns to the other side of the bodega. He finally grabs the handles of the cart and wheels it to the register to pay for the mound of items. The pieces of calabaza, the rice, the aguacates, the long pieces of malanga. Let's not forget his new floor squeegee, the impetus for this longer-than-expected Sunday grocery run.

JESUS IS HER ANSWER

They arrive together, a group of Pentecostal women with kind faces and leaflets in their hands. One of them, named Giseliz, towers over the others. Her dark shoulder-length hair is pulled back in a sparkly headband and she wears a matching shirt with one of the hermanas beside her. Their black shirts have a message in curved text: *Jesucristo es la Respuesta* (Translation: *Jesus Christ is the Answer*). Underneath the words is a globe with a cross in the middle. Giseliz approaches the register. "Van a la iglesia?" she asks me and the cashier. She wants to know if we attend church. She smiles then, revealing braces, and extends her arm to offer us each a leaflet. It is a single page, folded in half. The front has a black rectangle with white hearts along its edge. In the middle, a declaration in white: *Alguien te* AMA. [Translation: *Someone* LOVES *you.*] The message inside the fold, also in Spanish, insists God will forgive all your sins and cleanse you so you can be with Him for eternity. There's a rhetorical question in there: *No es asombroso saber que eres amado por Dios?*... [*Isn't it amazing to know you are loved by God?*]

Giseliz's goal is clear on this particular Saturday. She's here to "evangelizar." "To talk to people about God, because it's important to have faith," she tells me. "And more so in these times." She explains that the church they belong to is Pentecostal, but nondenominational. She and her fellow parishioners hail from different countries: Cuba, Honduras, Venezuela, the Dominican Republic. Giseliz herself is from Dorado, a town in Puerto Rico located about fifteen miles west of San Juan. Less than a decade ago, she left her island for Florida, joining a wave of Puerto Ricans who have settled here.

The relationship between Puerto Rico and the United States is incredibly complicated. The US invaded the island in 1898, during the Spanish-American War, and acquired sovereignty over it. The Jones Act of 1917 decreed that Puerto Ricans were now US citizens. But as a "US territory," Puerto Rico is neither a state nor an independent country. Social stresses and economic hardships drove Puerto Ricans from the island to the US mainland over several decades. Many have historically migrated to cities like New York and Philadelphia. Florida, too, has a well-established Puerto Rican community in areas around Orlando and the Tampa Bay.

At Giseliz's iglesia, there are families—fathers, mothers, and children. Giseliz is not a mother, though she hopes to be someday. She tells me she was recently diagnosed with uterine cancer. Scars on her abdomen tell part of her story. And her faith has helped her through. "I think almost all women—even if you say, *Ay, I don't want to be a mother right now*—you have that on standby. En espera. En la lista," she says. "Like, one day I'd like to be one, even if right now I'm not in the best financial situation, or maybe I'm too young because I'm in school, et cetera. For me it was like that." While Giseliz won't be able to carry a child, she believes God will grant her the opportunity to perhaps adopt one who needs the love that she knows she has to, and will, give.

On the subject of God, Giseliz acknowledges that there are people who may be uncomfortable if approached. She doesn't want people to feel pressured. Says she gives out pamphlets and encourages people to go to church. She hopes their faith will grow. Never would she go after people and tell them they need to go to church or else they'll end up in el infierno. "Eso no. Eso no." She shakes her head. "God isn't like that."

After some time, Giseliz lingers in the store. A few of the hermanas have begun shopping. The rest congregate outside. Giseliz walks around slowly, with leaflets still in hand. In the back of the bodega, an older man stands near an endcap. When Giseliz sees him, she perks up. Tilts her head and steps toward him. In a cheery tone, Giseliz poses a question. "Y usted, va a la iglesia?"

COMO LA FLOR

Katherine is undecided. She may make mondongo, a hearty soup made with diced, slow-cooked tripe and vegetables. That, or sancocho, a beloved stew made from different meats and various root vegetables. She takes her time walking down the aisles, scanning the items with her eyes and comparing them to the list in her head. Jorge, her husband who looms over her in height, trails behind with a shopping cart. He studies the many goods stacked on shelves from behind blue hippie sunglasses.

Katherine points out that meat is costly. "Inflation is extremely high right now."

"Yes, indeed," Jorge agrees.

"So it's really difficult," she adds.

The couple is here for some groceries. They've been coming to Orlando Latin Market for years. "They have the little Spanish stuff that we basically can't find in our regular supermarket," Katherine reasons aloud. "'Cause this is not really a—"

"Like Walmart," Jorge interjects.

"This is not an area where there's a lot of Latino stuff that we need," she concludes.

Katherine maintains that Latinos are accustomed to certain things. She stops at the end of the aisle where sugar and flour line the shelves. To her right is a rack of bright blue bags containing round milk cookies. She reaches for one. It crinkles in her grip. "Like this," she says. "I need some of these galletitas for the habichuelas con dulce that I make." Habichuelas con dulce, which loosely translates to sweet beans, is a Dominican dessert most often associated with Easter. It is traditionally made from stewed and pureed beans, milk, and spices. The milk cookies Katherine speaks of have a cross stamped in them and are often the finishing touch to a serving of habichuelas con dulce. Katherine herself is Dominican. She was born in Santo Domingo and raised mostly in Staten Island. Jorge was born in New York to Puerto Rican parents.

Soon the couple's cart carries a plastic-wrapped chunk of calabaza and tomato sauce. I ask them what these ingredients are for. What are they going to make? "She's gonna make," Jorge tells me. "I'm gonna eat what she makes." He laughs at his own quip. Says he doesn't have a choice in the meal. But he's good as long as he gets some.

They met in 1982, at a party in Manhattan. If memory serves, it was a Dominican baby shower. Katherine, then sixteen, remembers not wanting to go. She had just gotten home from her shift at a local discount store. She was exhausted. But her mother insisted they go together. "She said, *You're probably going to meet your husband tonight,*" Katherine recalls. "She said that, you know, playing around." At the party later, Katherine busied herself with serving refreshments to other guests. That's when she saw him. Jorge, dancing. He was twenty-eight years old, from Queens. And he was the party's DJ. "When I looked at him, I thought he was really handsome because he had really nice, thick eyebrows," Katherine recalls. "And that's what I first noticed about him." Jorge says Kathy got his attention—100 percent. "'Cause she was, wow. Like W-O-W. Like what's his name? It was like the guy in the movies—Jim Carrey—in that movie that was half-movie, half-cartoon."

My head is a gallery of images. I scroll through them until I picture the actor-comedian with a green face, his teeth like oversized Chiclets, his tongue wide and long, unfurling like a moist red carpet on a table. "*The Mask*?" A guess. "Bull's-eye," Jorge confirms. "That was my personal reaction. And that movie didn't come out in '82."

The kitchen was right next to the living room, so Katherine bobbed between both—filling up cups with soda before placing them on the table in the sala for children to grab. When the record stopped, she looked up at the DJ again. Later, as Katherine continued serving drinks, she felt a tap on the shoulder. It was Jorge, whose name is pronounced like 'George' by many. He asked her if she'd like to dance with him. She obliged. The first song they danced to was "Cama y Mesa," the merengue version by Fernando Villalona. In it, a man lists his many desires: to be a woman's silk duvet, the towel that slides over her wet skin, her lipstick. To be her good thing, her all. "We were just dancing the night away. He wouldn't stop dancing with me, and I liked his company," Katherine reminisces. "He kept putting on the records with one hand so that he wouldn't let go of my other hand." Jorge wrote his number later on a slip of paper and offered it to Katherine. She accepted it and said she would call him. But she didn't.

A few weeks later, a motorcyclist parked across the street from her sister's home on West 187th Street and St. Nicholas Avenue—where she lived at the time. Katherine's sister spotted him first. It was Jorge. "I knew she lived there, but I didn't know where," he says.

"My sister said to me, *Kathy, look who's there. That's Jorge.* And I said, *It is? Jorge?*" Katherine recounts the conversation. "And as soon as he heard my voice, he said *Kathy!* And I said, *Jorge!* And we kind of just took it all from there."

They would marry years later, at a Christian church in the Bronx.

"Do you see the ham, honey?" Katherine asks her husband. "It's usually around here." In the far-right corner of the store, they find a pack of jamón de cocinar in a freezer. The couple adds the cooking ham to their cart.

Katherine still hasn't made up her mind about what she's going to cook on Saturday. Soon they're in aisle 5, which is lined with bars of soap, powdered laundry detergent, and candles featuring images of saints. She points above her head, at a shelf with stacks of jabón de cuaba. The waxy multipurpose soap is quintessential in many Dominican households. "I was raised using this under my armpit. If not, I get grajo," she says bluntly. Body odor. "That's how Dominican I am." Jorge asks his wife if she wants to get a floor cleaner. On a lower shelf, by their shins, is a row of all-purpose cleaners from the famous Mistolín brand. "The purple one," Katherine decides for them. "That's the only one I use because these don't smell good at all." She gestures to the other colorful bottles on the shelf—floral, morning mist, baby.

"The purple one's the best," she says with authority. "It lasts longer."

"The lavender," I say.

"Yeah, the lavender," she confirms.

"Purple haze," Jorge says.

Katherine looks down at the cart and thanks her husband for getting a better piece of calabaza. The couple's attention then turns to sodas.

"Do you have the Kola Champagne?" Katherine asks.

"There they go in front of you," Jorge points out.

"No, this is the pineapple."

"That's the Kola Champagne."

"Get two Kola Champagnes, and get a pineapple," Katherine says. "Never mind, just get two Kola Champagnes. They went up to a dollar fifty. They used to be eighty-nine cents. That's how good I'm with this store, 'cause I know everything."

She adds two cans of Kola Champagne soda. They continue down the aisle and end up between bottles of seasoning and the wooden shelves containing boxes of root vegetables.

"Honey, do you want to get cornmeal?" Jorge asks.

"Oh, la arepa," Katherine says.

"La arepa," he confirms.

She considers it. Cornmeal is one of several ingredients needed to make Dominican arepa, a kind of sweet cornmeal and coconut cake. She ultimately says no, maybe another time. I then ask Jorge if his wife has taught him anything in the kitchen. He says she has. What's his favorite meal?

"I'm flexible when it comes to a meal. I could eat anything and everything."

"But what's the best meal I made you?" Katherine asks her husband. "You don't remember, huh."

It's sancocho. Katherine tells me she likes to make the stew with oxtail and cooking ham. And sometimes she'll throw in chorizo or pork ribs. Since her husband's late mother was Puerto Rican, Katherine says she likes to make her sancocho taste like pasteles en hoja (flavorful meat-filled pockets).

The couple's shopping cart has more than a dozen items by the time they're ready to pay: cans of Iberia tomato sauce, boniato, yuca, a bunch of bananas, Sazón Goya seasoning with azafrán (saffron), the purple Mistolín bottle, a cylindrical jabón de cuaba.

I ask the couple how long they've been married. They tell me forty-one years. Today, Katherine happens to be wearing a purple shirt bearing the title of one of Selena Quintanilla's famous songs, "Como la Flor." "At the time I had a Selena shape," Katherine says, her mind still in the past. "I really did. I had a beautiful body, everything."

I let her know she's still beautiful.

"Oh, thank you," she says, shyly.

Jorge looks at his wife with adoration. "I tell her."

YANICK OUTSIDE ORLANDO LATIN MARKET.

SOUP JOUMOU

Yanick stands in the corner of the bodega, before the commercial freezers. Her eyes focus beyond the frosted glass at the croquetas, cuts of meats, tamales, and banana leaves sealed in plastic. In her hand is a red basket with culantro and a bottle of Maggi seasoning, the nearly empty basket a sign that she has just begun shopping. Yanick stops by the bodega often—about every few days. "This is my store," she tells me. "My favorite store." It is before noon on New Year's Eve, and the woman from Ayiti is here to pick up a few ingredients. She wears a sleeveless black dress with patterns outlined in brown and white. Her short dark hair, graying at the root, is pulled back into a bun by the nape of her neck. Later today, Yanick and her family will head to a church service, to worship their God. "And after church, I make my soup," she declares proudly.

She will cook soup joumou, a hearty soup native to Haiti. The dish is typically made from squash, beef, a mix of vegetables, plantains, pasta, and spices. Around the world, Haitians consume soup joumou on New Year's Day to celebrate the country's liberation from French colonial rule. Because of this, it's also affectionately known as freedom soup. Yanick, who is from Port-au-Prince, Haiti's capital city, tells me her family loves her soup joumou. She points toward a row of large calderos—the kind for stews or heaping mounds of rice. That's the kind of cooking pot she uses. Tomorrow some of her family members will come over to her house to enjoy her stew—from the heart—with its potatoes, malanga, carrot, cabbage, and culantro. The meat, she says, will be prepped today.

Yanick is the main cook at home. "Only me," she says. "Only me." She is the queen at home. "I have three people in my house. My son and my husband—and me." She snaps her fingers. "Cook, clean—everything me." I ask Yanick if she ever gets tired. The inflection in her voice gives away the answer. "I'm tired always," she says, her rich laughter filling the aisle.

Today Yanick is pushing through exhaustion. She is brimming with excitement for the new year. She says God protects her life. "God is my father, my family. He's all for me and my family. God protects me." She places the basket at the base of the freezer door frame, by her knees, to free her hands. She mutters to herself as she turns a small package of frozen meat in her right hand. Places it on the shelf, then immediately picks it up again. Yanick is looking for the price first. She puts the package of meat back on the frozen shelf. "No goat meat," she says, mostly to herself. She picks up another package, from farther back on the shelf. Turns that over in her hand, too. "That's beef. I don't need beef," she says. "No goat. Nah. No goat. That's only beef." Yanick knows of other places that sell goat meat, but they are farther from home. Her eyes scan the shelves again. "Let me see here."

In Haiti, it is said that the enslaved were forbidden from eating soup joumou. It was a dish reserved exclusively for French plantation owners. Slavery, like in many other countries, marked Haiti for a long time. Enslaved Africans were brought to the island of Hispaniola and forced to work on plantations that produced indigo, cotton, coffee, and sugar. The Taíno, the Indigenous peoples of the Greater Antilles and surrounding islands, had also been enslaved, but their population was greatly decimated due to forced, brutal labor and various diseases brought by their Spanish colonizers. The French would colonize the far western portion of Hispaniola and give it a name: Saint-Domingue. It was here, in this French colony, that conflict began to brew heavily in 1791. That year marked the start of the Haitian Revolution, the most successful rebellion by enslaved people in the Western Hemisphere. Toussaint Louverture, a Haitian general and himself formerly enslaved, helped lead the way. Two years in, Louverture voiced this famous proclamation: "Brothers and friends, I am Toussaint Louverture; perhaps my name has made itself known to you. I have undertaken vengeance. I want Liberty and Equality to reign in St. Domingue. I am working to make that happen. Unite yourselves to us, brothers, and fight with us for the same cause." The Haitian Revolution would last more than a decade.

Yanick carefully closes the door, though it doesn't shut completely because her basket is in the way. She shuffles to the right in her black sandals and opens another freezer door. Yanick then picks up a new package of meat. A handwritten label below it reads, in Spanish and in all caps, RAVO ENSENDIDO. A misspelling that means to say rabo encendido—oxtail stew. She turns it over to inspect it. Places that back on the shelf. Indecisive, she rifles through the freezer some more until she picks up a new bag. Through the thin plastic, she studies the cut pieces of gelatin-rich meat, its marrow in the center. "No name," Yanick remarks, studying one of the labels. "Ohh, that's oxtail . . . Maybe oxtail." She finally chooses a bag and adds it to the basket. She turns around and walks over to a fridge at the very end of the back aisle. Opens the clear plastic door, reaches up, and points to a box containing calabaza. "You see this?" she asks. "Good. Good thing." She emphasizes how good calabaza squash is for her special soup.

In the 1970s, many Haitians fled their country for Florida's shores during the rule of the Duvalier family, a brutal dictatorship lasting nearly three decades. François Duvalier, known as Papa Doc, served as president of Haiti from the late 1950s until his death in 1971. His son, Jean-Claude (known as Baby Doc), then held the presidency until he was overthrown in 1986. Many Haitians left by boat, risking their lives on treacherous journeys. Haitian migrants were not afforded the same treatment by US officials as other migrants, like Cubans, for example. They were often considered "economic migrants," with many detained or deported. Those who managed to stay on US soil often faced anti-Haitian racism and discrimination. Despite the challenges, significant Haitian communities have carved out new lives in South Florida, particularly in Miami's Little Haiti neighborhood, as well as in New York and Massachusetts. The people of Ayiti brought with them their Kreyòl language, cultural traditions, and rich foods.

Next up on Yanick's list are plátanos. She rakes through a sturdy box of green plantains with her right hand. On this day they are two for a dollar. She digs her hands in deep and pulls out two before dropping them in the basket. Yanick prefers the thicker plátanos. The small ones, not so much. She swivels to a large box of avocados and picks one. Her small gold hoop earrings glint as she bends her neck down. Her polished nails—pink and glittery—move quickly like a spider's legs as she rotates the aguacate. Her thumb presses on it gently to see if it's ripe. All around Yanick, employees speak in Spanish. She places it carefully in the basket. Her hands are swift, efficient. "OK," she finally announces. "I'm done."

On January 1, 1804, Haiti became the first free Black republic in the world. In St. Pete, Yanick and other natives of Ayiti will prepare the same soup to celebrate the country's independence. This dish, full-flavored and big-hearted, makes her family happy. It's a taste of freedom.

NOT A JOKE

I find them at the end of aisle 4, next to the evaporated milk. Pink moscato and pinot noir in 750 ml bottles—the standard size for a bottle of wine. On the bottles is the word *Tetica.*

Te

ti

ca

There I stand, flabbergasted. *Tetica* is a diminutive of *teta.* To Dominicans, *tetica* means *little titty. Little breast. Little boob.*

My mom doesn't flinch. She reads it aloud. "Tetica."

"You're kidding me," I say.

"What does it say there?" she asks, sounding incredulous at my incredulity. Mami reaches out her hand and holds onto the metallic red neck of a dark bottle of Tetica Cabernet Sauvignon. She turns it slightly. The bottle has a pink label that reads *Tetica* next to the painting of a naked woman. I cannot make this up. Blue, red, white, and black brushstrokes form her voluptuous figure. The woman has east-west breasts. Her nipples are white.

"It's the competitor of, what's the name?" Mami says, pausing for a few seconds. "It's Culitos's competitor. There's a wine called Culitos. Did you know that?" I knew that, yes. Because years ago, while listening to 92.5 Maxima, I would crack up at radio ads of the Chilean merlot. A man with a deep, deep voice would promote the Culitos wine with its flavors of black cherry, chocolate, and raspberry. *Culito* means *little culo. Little butt. Little ass. Little rear. Little bounda. Little backside.*

"I know about Culitos wine," I say.

I check and see that Tetica is also from Chile. I pick up a bottle of pink moscato. Its label has the same painting of a naked woman.

"Mami," I whisper. "Tetica. It really does say *tetas* here."

She is farther down the aisle now, lining up merchandise. Nonchalantly, Ma says she hadn't noticed.

BARRIO BOYS, BARRIO BROTHERS

Papi and his eldest brother, my Tío Julio, say they had a good childhood in Santo Domingo with their brother Rhadamés (who we all called Tío Memé—rest in peace) and their sister Nancy (who we call Tía Morena). *It was a childhood where we worked, but we were happy,* my uncle remembers. *We received a lot of love. Mucho mucho amor.* My father says, *We were very happy because we didn't have internet. We didn't have cell phones. And because we didn't have any of that porquería that you have today, we would spend it playing, jumping. We would get together to tell stories. I loved going to el Malecón to watch the fishermen.*

Some of Santo Domingo's early barrios were located on unoccupied lands, near the edges of working-class neighborhoods. People made homes out of these informal settlements, raised their families in them. Over time, the barrios were transformed as reforms brought in cement construction, paved streets, and indoor plumbing. The barrio neighborhoods remained crowded, with children spilling out of their cement-block homes to play outside.

This is the barrio Pa remembers. He and his siblings, cousins, and friends were all very close. Julio would always look out for his sister and two brothers. *He would always protect us,* Papi says of his eldest brother. Tío Julio points out, *If I had to fight for them, I would.* My dad remembers how Julio would help him with his homework. *Sometimes—and he wouldn't show it—but I knew he would get frustrated because I wasn't very good at finding the value of x. He'd try to explain to me the value of x. He'd spend hours and hours and hours.* Pa laughs. Julio was very patient. *I had to be,* my uncle quips.

One time, Papi borrowed a pair of pants that belonged to Tío Julio without asking. *You had a suit for when you went to parties or somewhere important,* my uncle explains. *And he took my suit pants to do his welding. He took my suit pants to do that.* Later, Julio found the pants and slipped them on. *And when I went to put the pants on, they were filled with hoyitos.* The pant legs had many tiny holes, a result of molten metal coming in contact with the flammable fabric. *They were filled with little burn spots, from the welding,* my father confirms. They laugh now, but it wasn't so funny when it happened. And my uncle knew right away who did it. *Who else welded in our house?* my uncle asks, his question rhetorical. Pa still doesn't know why he took his brother's nice pants for the type of work that involves high heat. Says he was young—fifteen, maybe sixteen years old. He wasn't thinking about how badly that could go. *I wasn't thinking about any of that. I was just thinking about putting some pants on for work.* He laughs again.

Another time, my father took money from under my tío's bed to pay for a veterinarian bill. At the time, Papi had a brown poodle named Rocky, a very good boy who followed him everywhere around the barrio. One day, Pa was riding his bike when Rocky ran after him. As he chased behind my father, one of his hind legs got caught in a wheel. A panicked Pa braked and frantically scooped up Rocky. His leg appeared broken. Papi rushed home with his dog. *I had seen some money under Julio's bed,* he tells me. *He had about ninety pesos. At that time, ninety Dominican pesos were more than ninety American dollars.* Pa grabbed some of the money, hailed a cab, and brought Rocky to the animal clinic. A cast was put on the dog's leg, and Pa and his poodle returned home. My father placed whatever money was left under his brother's bed. When Tío Julio went to check under the mattress, he found he had less money than before. Much less. Pa remembers his older brother asking if he'd seen the stack of pesos. My father replied, "*Sí. Look at it here,*" and gestured toward Rocky. *He said it to me like it had been his money,* my uncle recalls. *What could I do?* No punches were thrown. No physical fights. *That was my brother,* my tío says.

My uncle asks me if I know what "marotear" means. I don't. It means picking up or eating fruits from another person's property. *You jump over, grab as many fruits as you can,* he explains. *That's marotear. Robar y marotear e' la misma vaina.* To steal and marotear are the same thing, he says. Tío Julio laughs. *Oye! In front of my house there were two mango trees.*

But no. My uncle had no interest in mangoes within reach. *We preferred to take fruit from other people's trees, because then you had to steal. It was the adrenaline, tú sabe.* I imagine a group of boys from el barrio—Black, brown, trigueño, fair-skinned, tall and lanky, short and stocky—hopping iron fences to steal fruit from strangers' yards. My uncle clues me in. *The fruits tasted better when they were stolen. They tasted sweeter. Mas dulce.* Papi disagrees. He said marotear and stealing aren't the same. *No robar,* he clarifies, his voice lilting. *There were many public spaces owned by the government, and they had fruit. And so you'd enter and you'd take it. But it wasn't illegal.*

My father, my two uncles, and their crews would often race each other around the barrio. My Tía Morena also had her group of friends. They'd play el topao, which Pa says is basically tag. *We'd pay el topao in the trees. We'd go from one branch to another, like monkeys.* They wreaked havoc. There was a place by el Malecón called la bolita del mundo, with a fountain. The security guard charged with surveilling that area raised fish in the fountain. *We would go there with our fishing hooks to try to catch the fish,* my father says. *And some of us would watch for him because, as soon as he would see us, he'd chase after us.* The memory bubbles up for my father, making him laugh. *We were tremendito,* he admits. They were a mischievous bunch.

There was also a man on the corner of their block who was known as El Viejo Polyester. That's what everyone called him. He had a fruit and vegetable stand. El Viejo Polyester also had a fifty-five-gallon metal barrel that he used as a kind of oven. The man used it to bake sweet potato, to sell. *And at night, when he'd leave, we would take the leftovers and throw them at each other. Not to eat, but to throw them. Poom! Poom! Poom!* Pa chuckles. He says El Viejo Polyester never found out who was behind the incidents. *But I imagine he thought that someone took them to eat. Because he would leave between ten and fifteen baked sweet potatoes and he'd find none the following day.* He laughs again.

The Castillo children also helped at their parents' colmado. As the eldest, Tío Julio says his parents had him working at the family colmado from a young age. *But look,* he points out, *era una esclavitud, because all*

from left TÍO JULIO, TÍO MEMÉ, AND PAPI IN A 1970S PHOTO.

of my friends would be out playing, bathing in the rain, flying kites, all that. And there I was, wanting to go out. No use. I couldn't.

El Día de los Reyes Magos, or Three Kings' Day, marks the day it is believed that the three wise men brought gifts to baby Jesus. It is often viewed as a marker for the end of the Christmas season, and it is a major holiday in many Spanish-speaking countries. One of the holiday's traditions calls for children to receive gifts. One year, Tío Julio got a new baseball bat. *Los Reyes Magos gave me a baseball bat,* he remembers fondly. But then he had to report to work at the family colmado. *I thought, "Mira eso [Look at that]. It's Three Kings' Day, and I'm here tending to the colmado."* Los muchachos—his friends—asked to borrow my uncle's new bat. He lent it to them. *The whole crew, from there to here, came back later to return the bat to me.*

But the bat was no longer whole. *It was split in two. They had broken it.* Tío Julio said they didn't know how to tell him, so his friends came as a group, a united front, to bring back his bat. *They were afraid of your reaction,* I tell my uncle. He confirms so. *I told them, "No problem. It's* OK,*"* he recalls. *But as soon as they left, I broke down crying, "My bat! My bat!" Ya tú sabe. That's the stuff of kids.*

They got into mischief and some trouble, these barrio boys. Now they got stories for days. But Tío Julio insists it was a happy childhood. *You know what happy is?* he asks. Another rhetorical question. *A happy childhood. That's what I lived.* So happy, in fact, that he's kept the same friends from back then.

My father says Julio was a very good brother to him. *He always was, and continues to be, a good brother. Muy buen hermano.* And Tío feels the same about Pa. *He's still a good brother. Mejor que yo. He's much better than me. And you can tell him I said that.*

BULLETIN BOARD IN APRIL

Let's Ship Things to Cuba

There is a mobile home for sale this month. In bold black letters, the ad reads: "SE VENDE MOBILE HOME. 3 cuartos, 3 baños, 3 camas, 2 refrigeradores, 3 microwaves." Three rooms, three baths, three beds, two fridges, three microwaves. Someone had written "TAMBIEN SE RENTA." Rough translation: They can also rent out the home. Someone later changed their mind, so it became: ~~TAMBIEN SE RENTA~~.

Several more ads are for efficiency apartments. There's a slip of paper stating a preference for one tenant. Water and electricity included. Available in March, as in a month prior. Another beckons interested parties to call a number, with a polite *Gracias* at the end. "Se renta un apartamento con luz y agua," reads a third. An apartment for rent, with electricity and water. Lists two different phone numbers. Yet another sign is for a two-bedroom apartment—everything included for $1,500, near Tropicana Field.

Did you know that you can send packages to Havana, Cuba? To be picked up at the airport. A bright orange paper lists the charges by the pound. "Misceláneas, medicinas, alimentos." Miscellaneous, medicines, foods. No electronics. Another flyer, this one from a real estate agent, insists she's here to help. And someone else had written, in cursive, a list of furniture for sale: "3 small tables for the sala, a dark violet carpet, 1 brown-colored futon with a mattress, 2 dark wooden bar stools, a vacuum cleaner, a mesa de cristal para television." If interested, call Juanita.

A FEMALE BODEGUERA

AMARIS: Mami, cuéntame. What was it like being a female bodeguera in the eighties, or when you began?

MAMI: Bueno, it was very difficult because first, it was Freddy, my husband, who was a bodeguero. I would always be alone, because for him it was always work, work, work, and work. He was an employee, then later we opened a bodega and I worked alongside him. And it was difficult because sometimes I had to take my daughter everywhere to be taken care of, and find who could watch her on the weekends. Because I worked seven days a week.

AMARIS: You worked seven days?!

MAMI: [Slaps thigh] Y cuando no?

AMARIS: I remember that—

MAMI: [Thrusts an aluminum foil pan with a handful of tostones in my face]

AMARIS: Gracias, Ma.

MAMI: Eat, eat.

AMARIS: [Laughs] I don't want a toston right now.

MAMI: Eat one.

AMARIS: I already ate one.

MAMI: [Shakes pan]

AMARIS: Mami, I'm trying to interview you. Thank you. OK. Enjoy the toston.

MAMI: [Picks up cell phone and starts scrolling]

AMARIS: Mami.

MAMI: Tell me.

AMARIS: You're on the phone.

MAMI: Wait. Let me. Where's this Bluetooth?

[Both laugh]

AMARIS: The what? The Bluetooth? Or YouTube? Mami, can we talk?

MAMI: My legs hurt from standing. I need to rest.

DAMARIS SLICES HAM
AT A BROOKLYN BODEGA
IN A 1980S PHOTO.

AMARIS: Your legs hurt from standing. This is all going in the book. Mami, I don't remember that you worked seven days a week, because you were always there for us.

MAMI: Bueno, when your father was an employee, I was home for a time taking care of you both. But then when you were little, we opened a bodega.

AMARIS: Where?

MAMI: In Brooklyn. On Newkirk. And I had to help your papá.

AMARIS: What was that change like for you? To go from being home with your children to laboring in a bodega?

MAMI: I wasn't always home. Before I was a bodeguera, I took care of viejitos, worked in factories. I spent a bit of time at home when you were kids, but not the whole time because I worked.

AMARIS: I do remember when you took care of viejitos. But tell me about how it was working in a bodega as a woman. How did they treat you?

MAMI: Who, the employees?

AMARIS: The employees, the customers.

MAMI: Bien. It didn't matter . . . Bien . . . What else?

AMARIS: What was New York like at that time?

MAMI: It was difficult because it's not easy when you start a business. [Chews a toston] It's not easy because you borrow money, and you have to pay that back every month. To grow a business isn't easy.

AMARIS: And you worked alongside Papi at this bodega?

MAMI: What do you mean alongside Papi? We both worked.

AMARIS: I know, but what was it like working with him?

MAMI: Good. When he would go buy merchandise, I would stay at the register because we didn't have a cashier.

AMARIS: What was it like being a cashier?

MAMI: Good. Sometimes working with your spouse isn't great. You grow used to it. It's difficult in the beginning. Because twenty-four hours with the same husband is not easy.

AMARIS: [Laughs] With the same husband. As opposed to a different one?

MAMI: [Grabs aluminum pan of tostones again]

AMARIS: Mami [Laughs] . . . Interviewing you isn't easy. Your mind is everywhere. You're eating tostones. You're on your phone. You're rubbing your knee.

MAMI: It hurts. [Finishes chewing]

AMARIS: Tell me more about that time, in the nineties. [Bites into a toston] How was it in the bodega?

MAMI: That time in bodegas in New York was very difficult because people were being robbed. Bodegueros would get robbed. But thank God I didn't have that experience.

AMARIS: Thank God. But Papi did.

MAMI: Sí. But in front of us, they killed—I don't remember his name, but across the street on Halloween, they killed a bodeguero.

AMARIS: A bodeguero?

MAMI: Across the street from us.

AMARIS: It was a robbery?

MAMI: [Nods head]

AMARIS: Ay, Dios . . . How did that impact you?

MAMI: Oh my God.

AMARIS: To see that that happened right there—

MAMI: I didn't want to work in the bodega anymore. I was very nervous. Because I thought, *That could have been us.*

AMARIS: But you continued working?

MAMI: Hay que trabajar. You have to work. Because who was going to pay the rent and everything? We had to open the bodega.

AMARIS: You're a luchadora. You're a fighter.

MAMI: Muy luchadora. Too much.

AMARIS: And how do you feel having had this bodega for so many years here in St. Pete?

MAMI: Oh my God, the beginning was also hard. But now you see the fruit and it's been worth it. Por ejemplo, tú salista graduada de aquí. If you needed something, we pulled it from here. Thank God, He's given us so much health. And the business has grown a lot from when we took it over. Muy bien.

AMARIS: Are you tired?

MAMI: Of what?

AMARIS: Of working.

MAMI: No, I—I—yeah, you sometimes get tired and you want your free time, but I'm not *tired* tired.

AMARIS: Did you ever think that your career would primarily be as a bodeguera?

MAMI: No, but I saw that Freddy needed me. To get ahead, he needed me and I needed him, because to carry a business alone is not easy. Even with employees, it's not easy. For example, if five vendors arrive and he's not here, I have to tend to them. If he's sick one day, I open the store. If I'm sick, he opens. But managing a store alone isn't easy. We have given up doing a lot of things we've wanted to do. Now is when we are taking more time off. But we didn't take time off before. We'd both come here in one car. We'd open and close together.

AMARIS: Wow.

MAMI: [Breaks into a snicker]

AMARIS: [Chuckles] Why are you laughing?

MAMI: Because you . . . In the beginning it was hard, hard. We both opened the store and we both closed. We were everything because we didn't have a cashier and we didn't have many employees. Sometimes I was in the caja. Sometimes I was in the carnicería. Sometimes I would serve food. I was everywhere. We gave up on a lot of things that we wanted to do to grow this business.

AMARIS: What did you want to do that you couldn't before?

MAMI: For example, my sister Rosibel would throw parties in her house and sometimes I couldn't go because I wasn't going to leave Freddy alone. She would host parties, graduation celebrations for her kids, and I couldn't go.

AMARIS: And now you can?

MAMI: Now, more or less, things have improved. Not completely, because when an employee is sick or on vacation, we have to be here. But things are a bit easier now.

AMARIS: Now you've been to graduations, to parties. Now you can.

MAMI: Yes, now. But before, no. And we spent many years without taking vacation. Pero mucho. Not like today that you, the youth, take five vacations . . . [Snickers]

AMARIS: But you have the advantage of being your own boss.

MAMI: Yes, but sometimes it's not good being your own boss. It has its advantages and disadvantages.

AMARIS: When do you want to retire?

MAMI: I don't know. Only God knows.

AMARIS: Only God knows? Every time I ask Papi when he plans to retire, he never knows. You're both in your sixties now. Isn't this when most people retire?

MAMI: Must be the professionals. You don't retire at sixty. They give you sixty-five years, and at sixty-five, you . . . There are people who work until they're seventy.

AMARIS: Mami, I see that you have worked so much since I was a little girl. I admire that a lot about you. Where do you get your energy from?

MAMI: God has given that to me, it's true.

AMARIS: You're going to cry? No, Mami, it's OK. Mom.

MAMI: But I feel really good that I've accomplished so much.

AMARIS: You're going to make me cry.

MAMI: I've watched you graduate. Fredito, too, has his job. I'm very proud of all I accomplished.

AMARIS: And I am very proud of you. You have taught me how to fight for my dreams, and to work hard. Because you have to work in this life. If you don't work for something—

MAMI: No one is going to hand anything to you.

AMARIS: You have to get up in the morning and make the effort.

MAMI: And what I say is, if someone wants something—like to live comfortably—they have to work. You think if Freddy and I were sitting at home, in our mecedoras, we would be able to travel?

AMARIS: And now that you both travel, you still only travel to the Dominican Republic. Explain that to me.

DAMARIS CLEANING
AT ORLANDO LATIN MARKET.

MAMI: [Laughs] Now that we have a house there, we have to go and receive the things we've shipped there. Things to prepare the house. I want to go to Santo Domingo because your father's birthday is coming up, and I want to go to Saona Island. He's also been wanting to sleep in the house. We haven't spent the night there yet.

AMARIS: You still haven't slept in your retirement home. I want that for you both. I also want to explain to you both that there are other countries besides the Dominican Republic.

HANGING DOWN

Step into the bodega, look up at the fine fissured ceiling tiles, and you'll see them. A butterfly with magenta-colored hindwings and black forewings. Another one is tan with pieces of metal welded into flower shapes on its wings. To your right, above the aisle lined with bags of dry beans and bottles of Cuban mojo marinade, are more metal butterflies clinging to the ceiling grid. Then there are the other decorations that hang down from the ceiling. Miscellaneous items that are not all that miscellaneous. They dangle from fishing lines around the register—eye-catchers for customers whose items are being rung up. Colorful parrots on perches. A wooden slingshot. A miniature mecedora—rocking chair. A ceramic cherubic boy holding and kissing the Dominican flag. Maracas painted in the Puerto Rico flag. A bottle. A güira, a beloved metal percussion instrument. A mosquitero. Ma says many Cuban customers buy the mosquito nets to take with them to Cuba. There's even a small, blue bacinilla—a bedpan. In the back of the bodega, by the rolls of toilet paper, hang two Dominican tamboras painted in the main colors of DR's flag: red, white, and blue. "Because this is a bodega Latina, I've brought things over from Santo Domingo," Mami tells me one day. Like a hand-carved wooden fish chime. Some of the dangling items are gifts customers have given her from home. "I've been given things from Ecuador. I've been given things from Colombia. I've been given things from Puerto Rico."

Look up, over the credit card machine, and you'll see a small brush and a razor. "That's to shave, look," Papi says, gesturing to his face. "That was used in the times of our abuelitos," Mami explains. "At that time, they didn't use shaving cream. They used soap." This was in the 1960s. Ma remembers being a young girl and watching her father shave his face. Abuelo Julito would take the brush, soap it up, glide the brush over his face and jawline until it was lathered well. Then he'd shave. He'd do this before he left for his job at a tobacco factory.

A baby caldero—a cooking pot with rounded sides and a tight-fitting lid—hangs over the floor behind the register, huddled next to a long brown tube with holes. A natural loofah. "You use that in Santo Domingo to wash yourself," Ma says. Not the whole tube, but in pieces.

"In Dominicana they call it by two names," Papi explains. "Musú and servilleta."

Ma interjects. "More musú, mi amor."

"But in la capital and in the south, they call them servilleta," he tells her.

"Ah, pero son muy fino—servilleta!" Ma exclaims. Meaning people there are refined, using the word servilleta instead of the more popular term, musú.

Behind the Boricua maracas is a stainless-steel round lunch box. Mami calls it a cantina. "This was when, in Santo Domingo—I don't know about other countries—my papá worked in a warehouse. It was like a factory. They would send you to bring him his lunch at twelve o'clock." Lunch was usually arroz, habichuelas, y carne—rice, beans, and meat. Sometimes it was Dominican spaghetti, with its olives and bell peppers. Mami's eyes linger on the cylindrical container—her soft smile a sign of nostalgia.

Neither of my parents are afraid that any of these hanging items will fall on them one day. "These don't weigh anything," Papi says. "The calderito may break your head, though."

RAVAGE

Papi was at work sometime in October 2020 when he received a call from his doctor. *She told me, "Señor Castillo?" And I said, "Sí, dígame, doctora."* She had news. It wasn't good. Papi insisted he wanted to know. Whatever it was. The doctor said the results had come back.

He had tonsil cancer.

Seconds stretched over the line. Papi's reaction surprised her. He didn't cry. He told la doctora that he would come out of this. *I was never afraid. No. Para nada.* A treatment plan was arranged. My father began chemotherapy and radiation therapy. He stayed home and stayed away from the business. My mother shared the diagnosis with their workers, including her sister Margarita. She tried her best to be discreet about it, told them en confianza. From that moment on, everyone stepped up. And Ma did what she could to manage the inner workings of a busy bodega without her media naranja, her other half.

For months, Pa quietly underwent rounds of drug solution dripping into his veins. His weight dropped dramatically. Fatigue trailed him everywhere. During treatment, he stayed away from the store. His absence loomed large at Orlando Latin Market. People, so used to seeing my father around, asked about him often. A carousel of customers every day asked: *Y Freddy? Where is Freddy? Dónde está Freddy?* My mother couldn't handle it. *In the beginning, I told customers he was on vacation,* she says. *Then I told them he was home.* And though the workers knew Papi was sick, Ma wasn't ready to open up to everyone. *I didn't want to tell them because I was very stressed. And then every customer would ask me where he was, where they were treating him.* The questions, she feared, would force her into a relentless loop. So she made the decision to gloss over the reality at home. She wanted to protect my father and her own sanity.

There were days when Papi wouldn't get out of bed. *I would beg him to eat,* Ma says. *He would tell me, "My throat feels raw—like burned. I can't. I can't. It's not that I don't want to eat."* In the early mornings, before Ma would head to work, she'd leave everything in order for Papi. She prepared him chicken soup often, then strained it with un colador. Made him broths, poured them into bowls, and brought them to him on a tray. All liquids, in hopes that he would eat. But Papi couldn't. Not really. Radiation had ravaged his throat. It was difficult for him to swallow solid foods, and it hurt to swallow liquids.

In the afternoon I'd go home and I would always tell him, "Let's go to the park," Mami remembers. *And we would sit there.* My mother would pack refreshments in a small cooler. She would eat a salad, and Pa would drink something. *The only thing I could drink was Ensure,* he tells me. *And sometimes it would take me nearly an hour to drink an eight-ounce bottle. It was sip—little sip.* Sometimes, they'd sit by the beach. *Y así,* she says. *That's how we'd spend time. But it was very difficult.*

Guilt tugged at my father. Pa felt really bad that he couldn't help his wife with Orlando Latin Market. *Your mamá had a lot of stress from the bodega. Managing the store, for one person, is not easy. Para nada es fácil.* The responsibilities that come with tending to the business are already a lot between them both. There are the vendors, the customers, and the employees to consider. *It's a lot of things at once. Imagine for one person. So I felt bad for her because I wanted to go to the bodega but, in reality, I couldn't.* Pa wasn't the same. He didn't have the strength. And Mami wanted him far from the store. *I didn't want him coming to the bodega and for everyone to see him like that. I didn't want him to stand before customers, because he was so thin that you could see his bones.* Ma insists she wasn't embarrassed by his appearance. But it was difficult to see him like that. She knows how people are. People would see him and begin to ask questions. Though Pa was kept away from the bodega, he'd sometimes help Ma by running errands for the business. *I would check the account on the computer. I'd go to the bank, in the drive-thru, and I would get money to pay the employees.* He could no longer do the bigger errands—just ones at the bank. *He'd wait for me at a spot across the street, to hand me the money,* Mami recalls. Pa says it was a gas station.

During those months, Papi missed the store. He missed its energy y el corre corre—the rush and constant movement from aisle to aisle, from back kitchen to front kitchen, from Tampa for produce and back to St. Pete to unload them. He missed joking around with his customers and insulting them for fun. *I missed working,* he says. *I wanted to be at the bodega.*

LA COCINA

ATENCION
EMPLEADOS
CONTROLAR EL USO
EXCESIVO
DE TELEFONO
WASH YOUR HANDS

previous PART OF THE FRONT KITCHEN IN ORLANDO LATIN MARKET, WHERE EMPLOYEES SERVE COFFEE AND HOT FOOD, AND WHERE THEY MAKE CUBAN SANDWICHES.

THE COOK

Darkness still envelopes the St. Pete sky when Alberto reports to work shortly after five in the morning. A cook on the early morning shift, he is the man responsible for the food customers will later size up through a curved glass covering. He lowers a plastic apron over his head, then ties it around his red striped polo shirt and over his black jeans. Keeps on his Atlanta Falcons strapback, which perfectly matches his clothes. "From the moment I enter, it's almost nonstop," Alberto sums up his shift. "It's ahí ahí ahí ahí ahí." It's an expression. He means the workflow is relentless. It's one thing after another. His is a solitary job for the first few hours of the day.

By seven o'clock Alberto is in the back kitchen, standing before a busy industrial stove. Tucked away in a corner of the store, this is a room most never see but which employees go in and out of throughout the day. The kitchen is small, with creamsicle-colored walls coated in grease, and an industrial stove and deep fryer that take up a whole wall. On the wall directly facing you is a stainless-steel working table, its undershelf filled with cooking pots and a thirty-five-pound case of clear fry oil. Wire shelves on the walls carry aluminum pans, a box of food service gloves, salt, and a nearly empty container of crushed garlic. There's also a tiny sink in the right corner, squeezed between the working table and a large-compartment utility sink. Here is where nearly all of Orlando Latin Market's hot food gets made. On this Easter Sunday, Alberto is singlehandedly monitoring two large calderos of rice in progress—one yellow, the other arroz congrí (Cuban-style white rice cooked with black beans). Chicharrones fry in a third pot. The pork rinds bubble and dance whenever Alberto lifts the lid to check on them. In the back row are more pots. An endless swirl of steam rises from a pot of Cuban-style black beans—a popular side at the bodega. The day before, Alberto had soaked the frijoles in water so they could soften before cooking. The pot of glistening beans towers over the rest.

This is just one portion of the work. On this day there is even more for the cook to do. On Sundays Alberto also fries empanadas, croquetas, and papas rellenas. The fried foods, when ready and hot, are destined for the heated display case in the front kitchen.

Alberto is self-taught. Born in Sancti Spíritus, Cuba, he never attended culinary school, never soaked up the knowledge of famous chefs through observation and practice. He breaks down his education: "But you know, sometimes you're single. And if you've lived alone, you have to learn to do everything." Including learning how to cook. "Apart from that, el cubano—all Cubans know how to cook," he informs me. He says this like an undisputed fact. "Men, women, everyone knows how to cook." If there are Cuban men who don't know how to cook, Alberto figures it's because they've had a more comfortable life than many of their compatriots. Maybe they haven't struggled as much. Maybe they've always lived with their parents. Maybe they haven't been required to learn. These are all guesses. "Those of us who have struggled and have been through things, we're obligated to cook," he tells me. "Sometimes you're alone. Sometimes you have a partner."

Alberto arrived in the United States in 2014 with his two children. His son later died in a car accident and he was left with his daughter, with whom he lives in St. Pete along with her family. Alberto has two grandchildren here, and a third grandchild in Cuba—the daughter of his deceased son. The proud abuelo says he's been working to try to bring her here, to be with their family. The first few years after he arrived in the US were far from easy. Adjusting to a new country as an older adult can be tough. "It was very difficult. I can't place the English language." He'd love to speak it fully, but it's hard at his age. He is sixty-two years old and knows only enough English to manage life. At times, Alberto enlists the help of his teenage grandson to interpret for him. But the language barrier aside, the cubano feels good here. His priorities are his family and his work. He's happy with what he does have. He insists he's happy to live without a lack of anything. "It's not the same as being

ALBERTO CHECKS ON THE FOOD
HE COOKS AT ORLANDO LATIN MARKET.

in your country, because you'd like to be in your country," he clarifies. "But things are bad there." Cuba, Alberto says, is poor. He points out the scarcity of food and the country's electricity crisis.

"No *hay.*" There is a lack. There. Just. Isn't.

By 7:25 a.m., Alberto has already fried a heap of crispy chicharrones and cooked stewed chicken and pork ribs. He tends to the arroz congrí and yellow rice. On the working table in the back kitchen is a large plastic jug of ground garlic. The day before, Alberto had chopped a bunch of cloves in a blender to use as a seasoning for meats, rice, and other dishes he regularly prepares. Another large container holds a blend of tomato, onion, and green pepper, two or three spoonfuls of which is used for added flavor. Alberto now readies four aluminum pans lined with parchment paper. In each pan are half-moon-shaped empanadas in neat rows. The dough is the color of ivory. To start, he places a few in the deep fryer and quickly turns over the bubbling empanadas with a metal tong.

Alberto's been working here for about five years. And in that time, he's grown accustomed to the relentless swiveling from pot to pot, from oven to fryer and back to oven. He learned to cook on his own out of necessity, after all. Out of being single, too. He has yet to find a partner in the States. "There are a lot of women who come here," I hint to him in Spanish with a smile and raised eyebrows. It is true. Women are everywhere in the bodega, of all ages and circumstances. "Ah, yes," Alberto replies, laughter taking hold. "Pero ya uno no está pa' eso." At this time finding a partner is not a priority for him. "I've spent many years single. You get used to it."

He walks over to the stove and lifts the lid of one of the rice pots. Steam billows up from the aromatic mound of yellow rice with pieces of chorizo cooked in it. Whether he likes his job is irrelevant. It is necessary for Alberto to work. "That's the life of a human being: work to live," he states matter-of-factly. "There are people who may love their jobs, but I haven't found them." He chuckles. "Because I'd love to *not* work, to have what I need to live."

Other employees arrive later. They, too, put on their aprons and begin butchering meat, pressing sandwiches, restocking items on shelves, and answering customer questions. By late morning, when Alberto wraps up his shift, he smells like fried food, garlic, and seasoning. The smell clings to his clothes and hat. The frituras of his labor—the chicharrones and rice and pork ribs and black beans—are now displayed behind the curved glass covering.

Customers line up for a taste.

CUBAN SANDWICH

The baguette-like loaves are made in a Tampa bakery, where they're picked up and nestled atop children's car seats in Freddy's pickup truck before traveling across the bay to St. Pete. Customers here can find the soft bread in a large cardboard box, positioned in front of the carnicería. Each loaf arrives double-layered: first in a clear bag, and then over that a paper bag bearing the flag of Cuba and the words: *Cuban Bread.*

In the front kitchen of the bodega stands Liset. Paper bags crinkle as she places two loaves in front of her on the sandwich prep table. It's a Saturday afternoon in mid-April, and she's taking advantage of this brief lull to premake Cuban sandwiches before more customers arrive. Liset inspects the first loaf, turning it over in her blue-gloved hand. "Esto no sirve," she decides. This loaf won't work. She shows off the middle. It has what looks like a gash in it. A mishap while baking in the oven. "It has a hole in it, so I can't slice it in half." Liset sets the loaf aside and selects a new one. She balls up the paper bags and tosses them in the trash bin. With a knife, the petite woman cuts the plastic sleeves off the loaves and pulls them out. She balls the thin bags and throws those out, too. She brings the first loaf all the way to the right—to the end of a big slab of black cutting board that is the counter. "You measure it," she explains, aligning the knife she's holding with a vertical etching in the cutting board. The knife is long with a serrated edge. She uses it to slice the bread. She sets the piece aside. That will be the first sandwich. Liset then slides what remains of the loaf all the way to the right again, and slices a second time. That will be Cuban sandwich #2. For the third and last piece, she snips just the butt off. "There are some people who like it with the end," Liset snickers. "And there are others who like it without." She cuts up the second loaf, then starts slicing each piece of bread down its middle to form two sandwich halves. Top and bottom. "Now we put butter."

Liset takes one look at the penultimate sandwich bread after slicing it. "Este 'ta flaco," she says. This one is skinny. She points out that Roby, the butcher, is also part of this sandwich-making process. He runs the ham through the deli slicer that is then used for the sandwiches. Liset teasingly compares the thin bread to the thin carnicero, who works several yards away from her at the far end of the kitchen. Liset chuckles to herself again. She digs a small wooden spatula into a container of butter located next to the other sandwich toppings.

A one-woman assembly line, Liset spreads butter on one bread half for each sandwich. She pulls a stack of sliced ham from the condiment prep station. Folds two slices and places them on one half of each sandwich. She adds roast pork to the sandwich, then Swiss cheese—sliced long and rectangular to fit the length of the bread. All this prep work is meant to make her job easier and those of the other women serving food to customers. Liset places three sliced pickles on top of the cheese. The discs look like oversized buttons, a pop of green atop pale yellow. "I'm preparing now, and then I keep them under here," she explains, pointing to the refrigerated space beneath her station. "And when a customer comes, all you have to do is toast it." Behind her, several feet away, is the electric grill used to press the sandwiches.

Liset imagines having to start this process from scratch in real time. Every time a customer requests a Cuban sandwich, she'd have to do all these steps. Over and over. Time is precious, especially when the line for hot food is long, and some customers begin to request food soon after the store opens. Which is why the kitchen staff always has a few premade sandwiches on deck. Liset grabs a bottle of mayonnaise and squeezes. The mayo squirts out, a line of fancy swirls, down each sandwich. That, followed by mustard. One by one, she places the left half of each sandwich—the half with condiments—atop the other half that has layers of ham, cheese, and pickles.

If you haven't already guessed, the Cuban sandwiches are popular here. "They must be made every day," Liset says, her voice all business. "Every day."

TO FRY A MADURO

Norma stands in the front kitchen of the bodega, peeling a maduro. The plantain is ripe, with black blotches and stripes on its skin. The blacker it is, the sweeter it'll be. She holds onto the skin at the bottom and pulls up. An effortless pull that reveals a naked maduro with soft, mushy flesh. Her blue-gloved hands work quickly. Norma holds the knife in her right hand, the maduro on the left. The skin, no longer useful, is discarded in a small trash bin by her knees. The ripened plátano is then tossed into an aluminum pan filled with other maduros. "Estilo cubano." Norma says her way of peeling maduros is the Cuban way—the way she learned from her mother. She pulls the next maduro from a cardboard box propped up behind the trash bin. She holds it in her left hand. "Like this," she explains. Norma cuts both ends. She slides the knife down the length of the sweet plantain. "The peel comes off whole." Pulls the maduro's skin right off. It falls with a thud into the bin. The maduro then joins the others in the pan. Norma peels the next one in five seconds, and the one after that in six. More than a dozen remain in the cardboard box.

Norma loved sweet plantains as a child. She smiles when she tries to remember the first time she peeled one. It was a long time ago. "By the time I was twelve or thirteen, I would help my mamá peel the platanitos. We loved fried platanitos, and I would help her."

Peeling maduros for the bodega is not a daily task because there aren't maduros every day. It can only be done when there *are* maduros. Green plantains need time to yellow. To blacken. To become sweet.

Norma takes an empty aluminum pan and sets it beside the one piled with maduros. She picks up the first sweet plantain and cuts against its flesh diagonally with a knife. She does so swiftly, in a matter of seconds. The slices will soon be sent to the deep fryer. "Customers love it," she says. Though Norma fries maduros at the store, she isn't as enthused about preparing them in her own kitchen. She'd rather buy them already cooked.

At the bodega, Norma regularly prepares food. She helps season chicken. She fries empanada dough filled with chicken or beef. The energy and desire to cook when she comes home from work is dependent on the day. "There are days when I'm up for it and when I cook a few things at home. Some days, no. There are days when, if I can eat out, I will. Or we order pizza, anything. Or I stop by Wawa and buy salad, and everyone eats salad."

Several minutes later, Norma carries the pan to the back kitchen. Alberto, the early morning cook, stands in front of the industrial stove, tending to a large caldero of bubbling chicharrones. In the corner are two deep fryers, side by side. Norma distributes the maduros evenly into both baskets. She lowers them into the basin. Submerged in oil, the maduros dance. Minutes go by and Norma is busy, so Alberto raises the baskets for her so the sweet plantains don't burn. They are now golden brown. Norma then empties the baskets into a hollow metal tray. Into the fryer goes a new cluster of ripe, fleshy slices. Round two.

Norma expects the first batch of cooked maduros will go fast. She says the customers only need to see them. "A lot of people like maduros more than yuca." She resumes her post from behind the display window to serve food in a to-go container for a customer. The maduros are still steaming from the fryer. The tray holding them has not yet been put in its place alongside the other metal containers of cooked food. But the customer sees the maduros and wants some. With tongs, Norma grabs a browned slice and, one by one, nestles each on the mound of rice. She closes up the container and hands it to the waiting customer.

TRAINING DAY

Liset stands behind the curved glass that separates her from customers. On this Juneteenth morning, the steam table displays white rice, yellow beans, yuca, carne de res, and more. And on the stainless-steel counter before Liset are three empty takeout containers. They are made of Styrofoam, so they flap from the fan blowing just feet away. It is shortly after ten, and Liset is in full work mode. The thirty-four-year-old has dressed her thin frame in an apron over a black GUESS T-shirt and light gray joggers with Nikes. She takes care of the latest meal order. Scoops some yellow rice with a large spoon into a container and places it back on the counter before picking up another empty container. "One with pork, and the other with chicharrón," she tells her new coworker, Nayví—a tall cubana with jet-black hair pulled back in a bun. After scooping more yellow rice into the second container, Liset looks up at the customer. "No beans or yuca?" she asks in a thick Cuban accent. The customer wants both. She nods and pours spoonfuls of beans in all three containers. Nayví studies how Liset digs another spoon into the tray of piled yuca, watches how much of the root vegetable, its yellow-white flesh softened from being boiled, is added to each container. Liset explains that it's a spoonful. She runs through the different sizes of the containers and how the meals are priced. She teaches Nayví, when a customer wants yuca alone, how much goes into a container and for how much.

The air from the fan makes the women's plastic aprons flap against their clothes. Liset's mahogany-brown hair is pulled back by an ivory claw clip adorned with plastic flowers. She and Nayví both wear hairnets. Small gold hoops hang from their ears. Once all the containers have yellow rice, beans, and yuca, Liset looks up again. "Uh, sir?" She tries to get his attention. "One pork?" The man tells her he wants pork for all three. "Three pork?" Liset confirms, nodding her head. "OK!" she chirps. The customer then places another order. As Liset fills up two new containers, she explains to Nayví how to serve the beans and yuca and bistec. Nayví listens and nods. It's her very first day of work at the bodega. She is a sponge, soaking up all she can from Liset. Soon both Nayví and Liset fill containers with rice, fried papas rellenas, empanadas, and marinated pork. "Que tenga un buen día," Nayví tells one customer, smiling from behind her mask.

Within minutes, a very large caldero is brought to the women from the back kitchen. In it is a mound of steaming yellow rice with guandules. Liset shows Nayví how to scoop rice with a small bowl, from the caldero into an aluminum pan. The rice will then be transferred from the pan into the metal container at the steam table for customers to see. It may seem inefficient, but it's safer than placing the huge caldero on the steam table container and risk burning yourself. Nayví's gloved hand holds the plastic blue bowl at an angle and scoops some rice. She then adds it to the aluminum pan to her right. Liset's back is turned as she retrieves some more aluminum pans from a shelf below the steam table. She stacks two and walks over to show Nayví. "Look," Liset says. She points to a crease in the top pan. She cautions Nayví that sometimes a small hole forms in the reusable pans. The oil from the rice then dirties the steam table and the servers' hands. Nayví receives the tip, nods, and continues scooping.

On this day, Liset is tasked with training her successor. She will soon leave her job at Orlando Latin Market. When she began working here in March 2023, it took Liset a week or two to grasp the job and workflow—the intricacies of preparing and serving food. "They show you all the cositas, and you continue to do the same thing every day, so it becomes routine," she explains. "Then you start to feel comfortable." Liset says taking care of the customers is challenging at times because that part of the job is in-person. "Pero bueno, ya aprendes." You learn.

Just then, Nayví and Liset turn and see a new customer standing behind the curved glass. Nayví pauses her work and approaches the woman. The order is for Cuban sandwiches. "Señora, buenos días!" Liset greets the customer as she leads Nayví through sandwich prep. "With everything, right?" Affirmative. Liset bends down and opens the door to the refrigerated space beneath their station. Nayví stands behind her, head bent, too. There, in an aluminum pan, are a stack of recently premade Cuban sandwiches. Liset gives Nayví the rundown. She grabs a sandwich firmly between a pair of stainless-steel tongs and walks the cubano to the press. She explains to Nayví how to monitor it. In the background plays "La Loma del Tamarindo" by El Gran Combo de Puerto Rico—a delicious collective of men's voices, the piano, the percussive güiro. "It'll start to soften and you'll press on it and more and more, ve?" Liset looks over at her coworker. "Then we flip it over. I'll show you that." The outgoing server then flashes a smile to the customer and tells her it'll be a few minutes.

Liset has been juggling two jobs: the bodega and a new job at McDonald's. She works mornings at Orlando Latin Market, and from 2 to 10 p.m. at the fast-food restaurant. She hasn't been working at McDonald's a whole week yet, but she already notices a difference. There's the food, and the language. Unlike here, Liset works with americanos at Mickey D's. While Liset speaks some English at the bodega, she uses it less frequently. "You know I don't speak a lot of English, but I am understanding it more or less," she says. "It suits me to work with americanos because the language sticks to me more that way."

Her days at Orlando Latin Market are numbered, but she doesn't yet know when her last day will actually be. It depends on the training. "Yo soy la teacher ahora," Liset says with a wry smile. She's the teacher now. Liset will show her successor all she knows, until Nayví has the confidence to work on her own.

Juggling two jobs, learning more English, all of it's been work. Liset's four-year-old daughter is in Cuba with her father, visiting family. When they return, Liset looks forward to her mornings freeing up. She'll be able to take her daughter to school and to dance lessons.

Liset's child is the main reason she's leaving her job here after a year and some months. She needs to change her schedule, to dedicate more time to her child. "She's pequeñita and needs me."

LEAVING A MARK

It is shortly before 9 a.m. on a cool Thanksgiving Day when the tatted Boricua in a black beanie enters the store. He scoops up a red basket from the stack near the register and begins filling it. A container of peeled garlic cloves, packages of banana leaves. Mark is in a great mood. He stands in front of the steam table already lined with trays of hot food. His booming voice carries through the store, over the merengue playing. The first thing you're shown here, he announces, is love and a precious smile. With his left hand clutching his cell phone and basket, Mark gestures with his right hand to the women in hairnets on the other side of the curved glass covering. "The señoras who make the food, Dios mío, God bless them," he says in Spanish. "Bless those hands that touch this food, because they make this food with love! Con amol!" Mark throws his right pointer up and brings it down like a conductor, for emphasis. "And you ask everyone here how they feel, and everyone will say, *Bendecido.*" Blessed.

Just then, one of the employees yells from the carnicería, pleading to have the song switched to something else. "She wants to change the music," says Mark. He walks over to the meat section of the store to confirm who it was that yelled. It is Dailin, a longtime cashier who does a bit of everything at the bodega. I'm certain I know where Mark is from, but ask anyway. "Are you Puerto Rican?"

"Sí, yo soy puertorriqueño," Mark confirms with a nod. He's from San Juan. "A Boricua. Proud to be Boricua—hanging out with my Cuban familia. I love them. Dailin, I love her even though she doesn't love me back."

Dailin, still in the carnicería, has her back turned.

"Dailin, tu no lo quiere?" I ask her.

"No!" she yells.

Mark doesn't skip a beat and tells her he cares for her anyway.

"Habla mucho, habla mucho," Dailin says. She thinks he talks a lot.

"*Habla mucho,* says Dailin," Mark replies as he bends down to select

MARK STANDS OUTSIDE CHICO'S CUTS,
RIGHT NEXT TO ORLANDO LATIN MARKET.

an avocado from a cardboard box. "That's why I sold her a car. Haha." He picks up another avocado. "Mira, así hay amol, con un aguacate." That's love, he says, with an avocado. Mark says he's always welcomed here with a smile and the food here, he believes, is made with love. He turns his attention to the rows of víveres—yuca, yautía, batata. "There's everything here. This store, de verdad, has always been blessed," he tells me.

On this holiday, Mark takes a moment to reflect on what he is most thankful for. "I come from the streets. I was an alcoholic. Llevo diez años que no tomo." It's been ten years since he drank alcohol. "I come here and share with everyone la filosofía that God put in me. Addicts and alcoholics can recover. You just have to accept it, and desire it from your heart. I'm enjoying the fruits of sobriety." Mark tells me he enjoys spreading positivity to others. And he loves his Latin food. His plan today is to make Puerto Rican arroz con gandules.

Several minutes later, he is in search of cilantro. Unfortunately, they are out. So Mark has to settle for cilantro's sibling—culantro, with its long, serrated leaves and stronger flavor. He places his two packages of banana leaves on the conveyor belt and, on top of those, two bunches of culantro. Next up are the giant avocados and the peeled garlic cloves. "I can't believe I don't have cilantro," he mourns aloud. "You don't know the pain I feel in my heart that they left me without cilantro. Ay Dios mío."

EL CARNICERO

A huge chunk of beef in plastic lay on the butcher's table. It is shortly before one on a Thursday afternoon, a busy time at Orlando Latin Market. The chatter of employees and customers blends with the melancholy of a bachata. Roby is tucked away in la carnicería, located in the corner of the bodega near where his coworkers in hairnets serve food in to-go containers. His blue-gloved hands work expertly, using the meat cleaver to cut open the thick plastic covering. "Esto es bola de palomilla de res," he explains. With both hands, the carnicero rips open the thick plastic and pushes it down around the meat, to remove it fully. From this you can make bistec—beef steak. Roby is to prepare this for his coworkers to cook tomorrow. He picks up the heavy ball of meat, easily several pounds, and places it on the carriage. Locks it in place. He turns the dial to select the slice thickness. But just as Roby is about to start slicing, he hears a woman calling for his attention. She wants something from the meat display case. He tends to the customer, wishes her un lindo día. The butcher then returns to the machine and pushes the handle away from him. Out comes the first slice of meat. It has a red and purplish hue, with a coarse marbling of milky white fat. Roby grabs it with his left hand and places it on the cutting board next to the slicer. "It can't be too thin, nor too thick," he says. Out comes the second piece. "Not too thin," he tells me. "Because then it softens too much when you cook it and falls apart."

Despite preparing and cutting meat all day, Roby does not tire of it. "I like meat," he shares. "I love chicken, pork, and beef. I really like fish, too. And seafood." Roby is from Ariza, a town located in the province of Cienfuegos, Cuba. He describes a beautiful childhood. "Cuba was better in those times," the forty-nine-year-old tells me. "We had more freedoms." He says he was just talking with a relative back on the island, who told him Cuban children today don't have a childhood. As a child, Roby remembers fondly all the fun he had outdoors. He'd wait for the weekends with great anticipation because that meant no school.

It meant he could play in the beaches and rivers. He'd go fishing. He'd also go hunting for pigeons and ducks.

Then, in the early 1990s, the country fell into a severe economic crisis known as the "Special Period." It grew worse when the Soviet Union dissolved in 1991. The time spent waiting in line for food stretched on. Dietary staples like Russian canned meat and German sausage were wiped clean. Milk, which had once been for everyone, was now reserved only for children under seven. "After seven, you no longer had milk," Roby says. He remembers that time as very difficult. Muy duro. The years that followed were not much better, Roby says. Every day was a struggle for many Cubans to sustain their families, to find clothes or new shoes for the school year. Roby found his way to the US a few years ago to support his family back in Cuba.

In 1963 Cuba's government made it illegal for Cubans to slaughter their cows or sell beef and by-products without state permission. If caught, farmers could face fines or years behind bars. Roby recalls how some farmers would kill their cows in secret. They had connections—people who would let potential customers know, *Tengo carne.* Beef was sold on the black market. It would be stored in cardboard boxes, transmitted by car or bicycle. Sometimes, Roby says, the carne would be delivered to people's homes in white buckets. As if it were anything else.

Here at Orlando Latin Market, Roby now works with beef every day. He's learned a lot, found ease in this work. He now knows how to cut meat, chicken, and pork for chicharrones. A stark difference from Cuba. In 2021, the island country announced it was loosening the decades-old ban on the slaughter of cattle and sale of beef and dairy. After meeting state quotas, ranchers would be allowed to do as they wished with their livestock. Back in his corner, Roby cuts a new slice of beef. Red and purplish. Not too thick.

MESSAGES TO LA BODEGA ON FEIBU (FACEBOOK)

Does the store carry . . .

Pimenta moida?

Betaderm?

Chicharrones?

Tamales?

Preseasoned taco meat?

Masa?

Crab rolls?

Ají amarillo paste?

Frozen lucuma pulp?

Gaseosa (soda)?

Hibiscus flowers?

Alcanfor, product of Honduras?

Jupiña soda?

Mofongo?

Recaíto and sazón?

Pasteles for Las Navidades?

Pernil?

Hierba Santa?

Chamoy sauce?

Fresh cactus pads?

Ground annatto seeds?

Mamoncillos?

Spanish bean soup?

Ají dulce or culantro?

Keebler Export Sodas?

Cuban sandwiches?

Panca cherry soda candy?

Coquito?

Medianoche bread?

Canned green chiles?

Iguana meat?

Tapas?

Cuban pork for homemade Cuban sandwiches?

Guineos verdes?

Sour orange?

Tamales, preferably pork?

Doritos Nacho Cheese seasoning?

Alfajores?

Mantecol?

Viandas congeladas para uno hacer sopa?

Sofrito from Doña Lola?

Guava with jelly?

Passion fruit pulp?

THE RELUCTANT BODEGUERO

My father's eldest brother, my Tío Julio, is a proud father of three, and an abuelo. He is often jovial and almost always boisterous. And like Papi, he's a longtime bodeguero. He's also an incredibly engaging storyteller with a deep well of stories. His accounts are long-winded, filled with hilarious asides, and punctuated by many an "Oye bien!" I always found it endearing, my uncle's habit of reminding everyone to listen up while he's recounting something. As if our rapt attention weren't signal enough that we were, indeed, listening. In 2010, while a graduate student, I lived in Brooklyn with him, my Abuela Ula, and, for some time, my cousin Merfred. Three generations in a third-floor walk-up made for some funny memories.

Decades earlier, Tío was a married man who had no interest in working in bodegas. Or so he says. But Papi, whose nickname is Pey, kept insisting. He wanted Julio to join him at their Tío Bobito's store in Brooklyn. *And Pey would call me and say, "Come! Work with me . . . Y qué sé yo qué." Bueno. In the end, I thought, "Well, working in a factory for three cheles isn't doing much."* By then, Tío's son, Ivan, had been born. His then-wife, Angela, worked, but Tío Julio himself wanted a better job with better pay. So in the end, my uncle joined my dad at the bodega. There, stories were born. They grew and practically told themselves. Tío has many stories from the 1980s. A total of six men worked in that bodega at one point. *There was always one who had the day off. One would be off on Monday, the other on Tuesday. There was something really funny that would happen, where if something broke or got damaged, the question would be: "Who was it? Who did that?" We would always say it was the person who was off that day. "Fue Fulano . . . Since Fulano couldn't defend himself."* [Laughs] *So on the day I was off, they would pin whatever happened on me. On the day Pey was off work, they'd pin it on him.* [Laughs] "*Oye! Fue Fulano. It was Fulano!*"

On days when they would order food from a restaurant, this is how it would go: Someone would call the place, then yell out the whole menu: "*There's bacalao. There's qué sé yo qué! There's this, there's that!*" The others would respond: "*Order this for me! Put me down for that. Order me the moro de guandules! Put me down for the qué sé yo qué!*" All except one bodeguero. His name was Darío, but Tío says everyone called him Verdugo. *He would always say, "Don't put me down for anything. I'm on a diet." Ta bien. Alright. So we wouldn't order anything for Verdugo, right? We'd all order our food. Pero que pasa? Well, when the food would arrive, here comes Verdugo with an empty plate. He'd pass by us—one by one—and say, "Give me a little bit of yours. Give me un chin of yours."*

Tío laughs and laughs at the memory. That was Julio's first job as a bodeguero in New York—around 1988, 1989.

We were brothers. Eramos hermanos. I have a lot of good memories from there. It was me and Pey, Verdugo, another one who we called El Chavo. We all knew each other. We are still brothers. We still call each other and ask about each other's families. Many who were once bodegueros are taxistas now. Ya tú sabe. It was a brotherhood. It really was.

HAPPY BIRTHDAY, PA

Calling Papi by phone on July 8 while he's vacationing in the Dominican Republic.

PAPI: Hi.

AMARIS: Hi, Pa.

PAPI: Como tú ta, mi amor?

AMARIS: Bien. Happy birthday again!

PAPI: Thanks, my love.

AMARIS: Are you busy?

PAPI: No, tell me.

AMARIS: I wanted to ask you a question.

PAPI: OK, tell me.

AMARIS: Do you miss the bodega?

PAPI: Sí.

AMARIS: Really?

PAPI: Of course, mami. I like my bodega and I feel good there.

AMARIS: [Laughs] OK. What are you doing for your birthday today?

PAPI: Nothing. It's going well. I'm enjoying my time here with your mamá. We're relaxing in the resort. I'm going kayaking later, around two.

AMARIS: Kayaking?

PAPI: Sí, while your mom stays on shore. It's all included.

AMARIS: Ahh, that's great. I'm sure Mami is going to be lounging because she never goes in the water.

PAPI: She told me no. She's staying out of the water.

AMARIS: Qué bien. Well, enjoy your kayaking, Pa.

PAPI: Ay, gracias, mami. I miss you all. The boys and ustedes.

AMARIS: We miss you so much. I'm sure everything's fine at the bodega, and everything is fine here. Don't worry, OK? Happy birthday again. And don't forget about us.

PAPI: I can never forget about you.

BULLETIN BOARD IN JULY

Cleaning a Restaurant

The ads for apartments and efficiency apartments for rent fill the insides of the bulletin board. A few are even posted outside and taped to the bodega's brick exterior. People are looking for tenants. Their mortgage must be paid and bills are due. One piece of paper reads: "SE RENTA EFFICIENCY. INTERNET INCLUIDO." (EFFICIENCY FOR RENT. INTERNET INCLUDED.) On the right side of the board, an ad that appears to have been cut from a notebook page reads "Se renta efice." It lists a number starting in 727, the area code primarily covering Pinellas County. Near the bottom, another ad keeps it simple: "EFFICIENCY" written in pencil, with a number to call below.

Do you like to clean? Would you like to get paid to clean? There's a bright green paper announcing that someone is looking to hire people to clean a restaurant. You can play an integral role in keeping the eatery spotless. At the bottom of the flyer, someone has written a number more than fifteen times and cut the sheet around each number. If interested, you can tear off one of the slips of paper and call. Another notice offers salon services, with pricing included for haircuts and color jobs. A haircut for a woman will cost you twenty dollars and up. Same for men. Children (ages ten and under) will cost you fifteen dollars and up. There's also an ad for a "Clase de Inglés." An English language class. It's free, in Largo.

Another ad is for a room for rent. Utilities included. There's a number to call. And a note at the end: "NOTA: Solo Mujer." Women only.

BOTTLED IN A BASEMENT

I call up Tío Julio a few months after our last call because I want to know more about his life as a bodeguero in the eighties and nineties. *It was a brotherhood, what we had. We were all brothers in the bodega,* he tells me. *If one of us couldn't come in one day, we'd switch the day with someone else. And if the person could cover the shift, he'd do it without a problem.* This brotherhood transcended the block to other bodegas. My uncle says that, if one store was missing stock and another had extras, the workers from that bodega would bring the items to you. *They'd bring it or say, "Come and pick it up." That's how things were. Una vaina bien.* A good thing. *Una vaina bien?* I ask. *Una vaina bien,* he confirms.

I am curious about the different jobs at the bodega. There is, of course, the cajero, the cashier who stands behind the counter for hours on end. Tío Julio tells me there were typically two workers. *Habían dos personas. There was no designated cajero. Whoever was closest to the register would be the one to ring up customers. The other person would stock merchandise. If there weren't many customers, you could take it easy, mark up items and stock the shelves. Tranquilito.*

My uncle also tells me about having to handle empty soda and beer bottles. *Customers would bring us the empty bottles. We'd pay them for the bottles, and bring the bottles down to the basement,* he explains. *And every week, one or two bodegueros would have to stop what they're doing, go down there, and organize all the bottles. Because the companies would come back and pick up the bottles. That money would go back into the bodega.*

Descending to the depths of the bodega was a kind of hell. It was scorching down there. My tío describes the basement as having un calor de "apaga y vámonos" (a "let's close and leave" type of heat). Un calor de 'apaga y vámonos' is a Dominican saying. Oh, and it was a problem when you had to tell customers that you couldn't accept their bottles. They'd say, *But I bought them here. I have a right to bring them back.* You had to assume that they bought them from there. My uncle tells me that, if the bodega didn't carry that brand, then the workers couldn't accept it. *The customers would go to the fridge and look for them—miraban y miraban,* my uncle recalls with a chuckle. *Oye bien. If you sold it to them, then you had to accept it back because it said, "Deposit: 5 cents." You had to accept it. If not, you were looking for trouble.* Five cents wasn't a lot back then, he says, but when customers would bring twenty bottles, that right there would be one dollar. *When they bring you forty bottles, now it's two dollars.* I say to my uncle, maybe one dollar could get you something at the time. *Of course,* my uncle replies. *It's all relative, cariño.*

Turns out none of the bodegueros wanted to be sent to the basement. *That's where there would be un lío,* Tío Julio laughs. It'd be a problem. A chorus of workers talking over each other, how one had to go last week, and that it was someone else's turn now. My uncle laughs harder at the memories. *Because it was so hot there,* he stresses. *The heat was—it was un ensayo del infierno, the heat that was down there.* A rehearsal for hell. A fan wouldn't do diddly-squat. That would just blow the hot air around so you can feel suffocated continuously. *We would turn the fan on but it was useless,* my tío recalls. *I'm laughing now at what were good times.* I point out to him how he is telling me about good memories, but also talking to me about hell. *Sí,* he agrees, chuckling again, *but now they're good memories.* I recognize this rosy retrospection. He sees them as good memories now, even if those moments were uncomfortable. He and his brothers in the bodega grew used to having to go down to the basement. Work is work. There was an understanding that you may not have to go down there this week, but you were expected to the following week.

In the basement they'd find a mess of empty bottles and cans. *And a radio, so you can do some dancing in between the bottles,* my uncle adds. I know Julio is a fan of boleros, so I picture him singing to their melancholic lyrics. But at the time, he loved salsa music. *La salsa vieja,* my tío clarifies. *And merengue. Because el bolero was for something else.* I ask what was that? He tells me the bolero is for when you were in love. We laugh. I ask my uncle what kind of salsa he was into back then. *I am going to tell you. I'll tell you in order of my taste. Ismael Rivera. They called him El Sonero Mayor. He served prison time and everything. There was Héctor Lavoe, who you know about. His story came out in a movie and everything. There was also la Fania. The director was a Dominican named Johnny Pacheco. He would get all the artists of Fania together. Bueno, there was Ismael Miranda. There was Roberto Roena. A bunch of people I can't think of now.* I point out, *Tío, although you say it was hell down there in the basement of the bodega, you also had fun because you were listening to your music.* Yes, he says, so it would keep his mind off the heat that engulfed him. *Somehow we had to forget that we were messing with those bottles.*

Whoever's turn it was to sort through the bottles on any given week would keep the basement door open. They would place milk crates around the open metal door so that passersby wouldn't dare get close and fall in. *So they wouldn't fall into hell with you,* I joke to Tío Julio. Affirmative. I then ask him if a customer or someone walking by ever accidentally fell through the basement door. *No, no,* my uncle tells me. *I would have liked someone to fall in, though, so I could laugh a little.*

WE OUTSIDE

ORLANDO
LATIN MARKET
BODEGA LATINA 521-4545
LATIN FOODS TO GO DELI-MEATS & GROCERIES
Original CUBAN SANDWICHES BREAKFAST & LUNCH
3515
OPEN
Reddyice
Reddy

previous THE OUTSIDE ENTRANCE OF ORLANDO LATIN MARKET.

JUAN THE BOSS

Orlando Latin Market's double door has signs taped on it. One lists the bodega's hours: Monday through Friday, 8 a.m.–7 p.m., and Saturday and Sunday, 9 a.m.–4 p.m. A notice from the Department of Business and Professional Regulation Division of Alcoholic Beverages and Tobacco reads: "It is unlawful for anyone (including parents) to sell, give or serve alcoholic beverages to a person under 21 years of age." Another paper sign, written in black marker, reads: "TENEMOS MORCILLA BORICUA." Translation: WE HAVE PUERTO RICAN BLOOD SAUSAGE. And a few feet away from the door stands Juan with his own kind of sign, but one that can fit in his palm: a stack of business cards. It is a sweltering August day, so he doesn't plan on staying here for very long. Customers filter in and out of the bodega, the door its own kind of Rolodex. As they enter, the tall and slender Juan offers them his card. He lets them know he's a Realtor. If they or anyone they know needs to buy or sell a home, they can give him a call. "I make it quick," Juan tells me later. "I don't want to be in their way either, because I know that they want to go in and out." Some stay to talk. Others take the card and keep it moving.

This outreach has worked for Juan. He's been going to Orlando Latin Market for several years now and says he's been able to get clients this way. From the bodega he gets mostly Latinos interested in working with him. Generally speaking, he says, the great majority of them desire a single-family home. About 99 percent of them, to his estimate.

Juan has been a Realtor for over thirty years. And in that time, he's witnessed many changes to the market. "I've been through everything, so I'm kind of immune to any changes now. I've been through the good, through the bad, through the highs to the lows."

The most rewarding part of Juan's job is fulfilling the dreams of families who never thought they could own a home. "I like the freedom. I don't have to punch a timecard," he adds bluntly. Juan's work gives him ample time for travel. He's been to England, France, the Netherlands, Germany, Switzerland, Italy, Spain, Portugal, Greece, Turkey, Israel, Jordan. He says he's headed to the Caribbean next. "I'm my own boss."

MOLINA STANDS OUTSIDE
ORLANDO LATIN MARKET.

A SOMBRERO ALWAYS, SIN PENA

Molina is a giant at six foot two. He towers over his petite wife and over a good number of people. Age has deepened his frown lines, but his eyes remain kind. The seventy-six-year-old is a self-described guajiro—a cubano from the countryside. The telltale sign is not the button-down shirt and slacks that form his daily attire. It's the sombrero he wears every day. Molina owns about a half dozen of the wide-brimmed hats. They can be found in his St. Petersburg home, stacked on top of an old dresser, high up so no harm can come to them. "The sombrero is part of my life," he says plainly. "To me, the sombrero is almost sacred."

Molina wears one of his oldest cowboy hats to the bodega one Saturday in late March. It's an aged tan sombrero made from beaver fur. Above the braided band is an archipelago formed from his sweat. Tan turned brown, like watercolor bleeding on paper. Molina has owned this Stetson for years. He purchased it from a sombrerería in Miami. The visit to the bodega with his wife is meant to be quick. They're here for some dish soap. But it's difficult to slip in and out of an establishment you used to work at. People notice the sombrero. They recognize the guajiro with the salt-and-pepper hair poking out from underneath it, and their eyes light up. A revolving door of people wants to catch up with Molina: Tía Margarita, his former boss, Freddy, and other customers.

"Muchacha!" Molina calls out to a woman. "Cómo anda'?"

She gives him a big smile. "Qué bueno verlo!" she replies.

Outside the store, Molina acknowledges a younger man and asks, "Cómo está la cosa?" He wants to know how life's going, to which the man replies, "Todo bien." All good. Just about everyone peers up at Molina and his sombrero, with its crown and dents and middle crease. The broad-brimmed hat is akin to a limb for him. He surmises that, if he removes his sombrero, it'd be as if he were shirtless. "I've always, always, always had a sombrero," he says. "From when I was a boy."

Let us imagine Molina, born in 1948, during a period of democracy in Cuba that was also rife with corruption. The 1940s in Cuba were a time of large sugar harvests, the largest the country had seen in decades. Fulgencio Batista, who had previously served as an elected president, staged a coup and took over the country in 1952. In the years that followed, Fidel Castro began working toward his revolution, which he achieved in 1959.

But that is still in the future. Let's imagine Molina as a child from the small village of Cabañas on the northern coast of western Cuba. Long before people called him by his last name, he was the son of an agricultural worker father and a mother who carried the weight of their home and raised him and his sister. When Molina was about five or six, he was gifted his first sombrero. "My mamá would tell my papá, *We need to buy a sombrerito for el niño, for the sun.*" He unfurls the memory, chuckles at it. Molina says he and his peers would all wear little sombreros to school. At home, he'd switch on another sombrero to help his father tend to the cows and other livestock.

The sombrero stayed on as he grew. Molina was about twelve years old when he began assisting his father in the sugarcane fields. In times of zafra—harvest—he would only go to school part-time. He remembers wanting to help his parents. "Because I saw they worked so much, you began to help. To work."

Time went on. Molina grew into adulthood. High-quality sombreros were hard to find in Cuba. "I had three there," he tells me. "They call them Tejana." On the island, he carved out a life with his wife and their three children. Fidel Castro's Communist Party, which came to power decades prior in the 1959 Cuban Revolution, controlled many aspects of Cuban life, from media to the arts and religion. This control led to the persecution of religious groups like Jehovah's Witnesses. In 1974, the sect was banned in Cuba. In a December 1976 report for *Worldview,* political scientist Frank Calzon wrote that the Cuban government's official campaign against the Jehovah's Witnesses in Cuba had developed swiftly over just a few years. Citing *Granma,* Cuba's state-run newspaper, he reported that the country's First National Congress on Education and Culture in 1971 approved a resolution stating that "obscurantist and counterrevolutionary sects must be unmasked and fought." Jehovah's Witnesses, among other major sects, were to be watched closely due to their allegedly counterrevolutionary activities, Calzon wrote.

Molina is a Jehovah's Witness. The persecution of Witnesses in Cuba was the main reason why he and his family left Cuba for the United States in 1994. He had been made by the government to work in a UMAP, which stands for Unidades Militares de Ayuda a la Producción (translation: Military Units to Aid Production). UMAP was a system of agricultural forced-labor camps operated by the Cuban government that targeted people who opposed Castro or who would not conform to the status quo. This included members of the LGBTQ+ community, Catholics, and Jehovah's Witnesses like Molina. He says he served time in UMAP before prison. "In the camp they'd punish me. It was all a desatino," Molina recalls. Foolish. Nonsensical. "Sometimes they'd give you food, sometimes not. They'd make you, or try to make you, march like military men, as if you were training."

Molina maintains he was never afraid to be a Jehovah's Witness, freely, unapologetically. He remains one today.

When he arrived in the United States decades ago, one of the first things he did was search for a new Texan-style sombrero. He bought his first one in Miami. Molina is far from rich, but he likes a top-quality sombrero. He wears one to the rodeo and to concerts, to the supermarket, on any errand. If he goes to the hospital, expect to see him in a sombrero. Molina's son, Ibrahim, grew up watching his dad don this hat everywhere. "*Here comes John Wayne and his son!* And of course as a kid, you're like, *Jesus, Dad. Why are you going to wear a sombrero?* But now you realize what he was doing—expressing himself in a way that didn't have to communicate a lot."

Guajiro!

Guajiro!

Guajiro!

When other Cubans see his father out in public, that's what they call out. "Everyone knows him. *Oh, el guajiro!*" Ibrahim explains. "The tall Cuban. Because he's pretty tall for a Cuban. We don't come that size. He's not standard." He admires how unapologetic his father is. He says Molina has never let the unpopularity of a subject detract him from sharing it, or from changing who he is. "He doesn't care what you think of his hat," the proud son says. "He's gonna wear that sucker everywhere."

Yes, this guajiro will continue to wear his sombreritos. His sombreros. "There are people who have told me, *I'd love to use a sombrero, but I'm embarrassed,* because they think they'll be categorized as guajiro—like a person from el campo," Molina says. "I'm not ashamed of that. That I came from a poor man, and from el campo puro, is everything. No me da pena."

MADRE E HIJA, HIJA E MADRE

The inseparable pair stops by Orlando Latin Market one Saturday morning in late April. As they have many times before, Barbara and her older daughter, Brisas, make their rounds. The bodega is an old stomping ground for them. They've been shopping here for years. Back then, Brisas was a precocious little girl who loved to talk, and the owners and employees delighted in her visits. On this day, mother and daughter greet the workers, then head next door to the coin laundromat. Their clothes have been washed and dried and now need to be folded. Sounds fill the laundromat. A reggaeton song plays in the background. Wet, soapy clothes churn in machines. "How would I describe my relationship with my daughter?" Barbara repeats my question as she looks over at Brisas. "She's like the sister I never had." Her tall and slender eighteen-year-old listens quietly, folding each article of clothing and adding it onto neat piles on the table. Barbara's own parents had five children. Four boys, one girl. Years and years later, "God gave me the opportunity to have daughters," she says. Barbara had two girls—Brisas and her younger daughter. Brisas means "breezes" in Spanish. Before she had children, Barbara always knew she liked the name for a girl. In Cuba, there is a hotel called Brisas del Mar. "I visited as a girl, and I liked the name. Brisas."

The mother and her daughters have weathered many storms. Barbara and her partner separated, and just like that, it became her and her two girls. "Being a mother, for me, is everything. It's everything to me. It's learning how to be a sister, learning how to be a friend," she says. "I'm not one to have a lot of friends, so my daughters are everything to me." Her eyes grow teary. "It's a beautiful thing. Every day I experiment and continue to learn."

Barbara believes the most difficult part of motherhood is not having more family around them. To date, only her father and one of her brothers are here in the United States. Her mother remains in Cuba. It's a struggle to keep pushing forward with her daughters, alone. This is why she likes coming to the bodega. There she feels the closeness of family. Barbara says Freddy has shown her the support of a father. "And since very young, my girls have loved Freddy like an abuelo. That makes me proud. They feel like they have family." Barbara has dreams for her life. She wants her daughters to study, to graduate. Someday, too, she'd like to own a home. A four-bedroom house with a big backyard. She'd love to travel, which she says she can't do now because she's a mother. But once her daughters flourish, she wants to see other parts of the world.

Brisas's best friend is her mother. "But at the same time, she's my teacher 'cause she's showing me everything. She already went through everything, so she's the one showing me how to handle different paths. She's all I got." Brisas goes to her mami whenever she needs help and whenever she needs to talk to someone. "She's my everything. She's my teacher," Brisas says, her voice breaking. "I like to tell people, *Ella es mi Diosito. Mi reina.*"

Barbara looks at her daughter, her own eyes glassy with tears. "That's what she calls me," she confirms. Now they both have me crying.

In the past, mother and daughter have had issues with communicating their emotions. Both have major stressors in their lives. Barbara is a single parent, and Brisas is a student who dreams of becoming a pediatrician someday. "But now we're at a place where we both realize that it's just us against the world, and we just gotta talk," Brisas points out. "We gotta go through it. She has to understand me. I have to understand her."

Barbara and Brisas think the same, crack the same jokes, have the same taste. They even wear the same size clothes, as evidenced in their piles of clean laundry. "We're the same person," Brisas says with an amused smile, "just in different bodies." For Barbara, the most beautiful part of motherhood is knowing that her girls are a part of her. "I wouldn't want anything to happen to them." Her voice quivers again. "I'm very protective. I love them a lot. They're the greatest thing I have. They're my family. The family I created."

A PALLET OF DREAMS AND BEANS

Freddy drives his black pickup truck down a two-lane road in East Tampa, past residential homes and a cemetery. It is Friday the Thirteenth, and he's on his way to pick up an order from one of his longtime suppliers. It's a long drive from home, easily more than forty minutes.

He arrives at 8:15 a.m. He slows the truck and stops in front of a chain-link fence topped with barbed-wire arms as tall as his vehicle. Beyond the fence is an ivory-colored building bearing the name of the business that imports and distributes food products like the kind Freddy sells. I'm waiting for my father in the parking lot. He honks the horn. It blares. Almost immediately, the gate opens to a loud screech. Freddy turns right and parks his truck parallel to the fence. When he steps out, I see he's wearing loose gray joggers and black sneakers. Ocean waves cover his long sleeve shirt from the Habit brand.

In front of the big warehouse stand two employees, tending to another customer. They greet Freddy. He does this trip weekly, so he is swift. He opens the tailgate and picks up a flattened cardboard box lying on top of other miscellaneous items, tosses it to the ground, and begins clearing the truck bed. He needs to make room for the wooden pallet carrying the merchandise he had asked for. It's a big order. Nesquik chocolate powder. Large yellow cans of Sultana soda crackers. Inca Kola. Four fifty-pound sacks of black beans. One of the workers sees me filming my father and asks if I'm taking a picture to make sure that Freddy works. He jokes that ese tipo—that guy—doesn't work. My dad doesn't say anything, just chuckles and brushes dirt off his hands. Cooking wine from La Trigueña. A box containing a dozen seven-day yellow candles. Sour orange marinade from La Lechonera.

A boat anchor sits in the middle of the truck bed, near a wrench. Freddy stoops down to pick both up and stores them in his truck toolbox. Once the bed is mostly cleared, he steps down and returns

FREDDY LOADING UP
A BOX OF BURRO BANANAS
IN TAMPA FOR HIS BUSINESS.

the flattened piece of cardboard. He walks to the driver's side and prepares a check.

"You got a black pen?" he asks me.

"I do, I do. Yep."

I hand him one.

He asks for today's date. I remind him it's September 13th. He dates the check but can't remember what the total is. He'll get that soon enough.

A worker operating an electric forklift approaches with the pallet. On it sits Freddy's order—cans of soda crackers on top of sacks of black beans on top of boxes, all wrapped tightly in layers of plastic. An oddly shaped block of considerable size. The man steering the forklift cranes his neck to the left for a better view of what is before him. Freddy points his finger toward the truck, as a signal to keep going. The man slows to a stop. Papi gives him a thumbs-up. As the forks lower the pallet onto the truck bed, Freddy leans forward to see where it will be placed. The man backs up, leaving the merchandise on the open tailgate. The black truck sags under the new weight. The worker then inches forward again, using the forks to lift up one side of the heavy pallet. The forklift gently pushes the pallet farther into the bed.

"Ahí esta bien. Perfecto," Freddy tells the man. The pallet is perfect there. The forklift beeps as the operator backs up. My dad jokingly warns the worker not to scratch the vehicle. "That truck belongs to my wife." He then lifts the tailgate, closes it shut.

"Vamo' a ver, primo," Freddy says. He's ready to pay what he owes. He climbs back into the driver's seat. Another worker brings him an invoice. Freddy reviews the itemized sheet and pays.

Before my father heads out, a smile spreads on his face. "I'm a lazy guy," Freddy says to the warehouse employees, referring to the earlier joke about him as a do-nothing. "I don't work." It is now shortly before 8:30 a.m. The gate reopens. Freddy drives off, his truck now much heavier.

WELCOME TO CHICO'S CUTS

Make a right from US 19 onto Thirtieth Avenue North and you'll notice a barbershop right before Orlando Latin Market. It has no awning, but a tinted glass wall bears the name, CHICO'S CUTS. Below are more words in blue—a beacon for Spanish speakers: TU BARBERO LATINO (YOUR LATINO BARBER).

The barber inside the shop is the owner, Chico. That's what most people call him, but his real name is Alexander. At the bodega, he's got a lesser-known nickname: Gullo. Chico's got a calm disposition about him. He has tattoos, rocks diamond studs in his ears, and keeps his own head closely shaved. He is also a longtime customer at the bodega, stopping almost every morning for espresso and around noon for hot lunch between appointments.

One Thursday morning in late February, Chico puts on gloves and prepares his clippers for the next haircut. His second client of the day is one of his regulars. Mark, a local car salesman. It is Mark's day off and the puertorriqueño wants the usual: a medium skin fade, three on top. Chico sits his client down all the way to the right of the shop, in the first of four chairs. The barber then places a black polyester cape around his neck. It drapes over Mark's body, revealing only his sandals at the bottom.

To the right is a flat TV hanging on a red wall. The barbero often looks up music on YouTube, searching for songs that match the taste of his regular clients before they arrive. Sometimes he plays opera for Mark. But on this day, Chico opts for R&B. "Just good vibes," he says. Mark agrees. Chico's left hand holds onto Mark's head to keep him still. His right hand holds the clippers, buzzing off his client's hair close to his scalp. Mark now faces the TV. "You can't go wrong with that, right?" Chico asks, referring to the genre. His client cosigns, but makes sure not to nod in agreement. Can't risk messing with his fade. The barber glances to his left at the TV for a second. On the screen is a music video.

Four Black men in crisp white suits are singing. "That's nineties music, man," Chico says. "The best."

"Who's that?" Mark asks. "Boyz II Men?"

"Yeah," Chico responds.

For the next few seconds, the men are silent as a bespectacled Nathan Morris sings about moving on after a heartbreak. The singer wears a tan shirt and white dress pants with a light brown belt. "They used to even dress better at that time," Mark observes aloud. "Look at that. Pleated pants. The suits. I'm for real." The gold on Chico's teeth glints as he smiles. He looks back at the TV to see what his client sees. He then steps away from his client to brush off his clippers. Attaches a clipper guard and returns to the work at hand.

Mark has been going to Chico's Cuts for about five or six years. He thinks not enough people give credit to barbers for all they do. "Barbers are like bartenders. They're like psychologists. They're like therapists. You come in here and you sit, and you're going through some things in life. Guess who hears you?" Chico's gloved right hand runs the clippers up and down quickly, creating a smooth blend. "The barber," Mark answers his own rhetorical question. "The barber gives you his opinion. Sometimes you come in here for a haircut, and you leave with not only that. You feel better emotionally, mentally, physically. You know what I'm saying?"

—

Before Chico acquired this space in December 2014 and turned it into a barbershop, it had been a women's clothing boutique. What attracted him the most about this particular location was the parking. He didn't want his shop in a plaza, with those pylon signs that list all the tenant businesses that motorists can miss. "You can just drive by here and look over here, because I'm by myself," he explains. "You're gonna see me, that it's a barbershop."

It took time to make it his. Chico's Cuts is clean and tidy, with cream square tile flooring and red- and ivory-painted walls. When customers walk in, they'll see four red-and-black barber chairs. Before each chair is a rectangular mirror on the wall. To your immediate left is a row of foldable black chairs and an ATM machine in the far corner. A sepia-tinted window overlooks a few parking spots between the shop and Orlando Latin Market. And hanging from the red wall beside the window is a Cuba jersey from the 2013 World Baseball Classic. Rolando Arrojo, a retired Major League Baseball pitcher, had signed it and gifted it to the barber. The jersey is a nod to Chico's Cuban roots. He was born in Mariel, Cuba, and left for the United States at fifteen years old.

Chico occupies the chair to the far right of the shop. His tools and clippers are arranged neatly on his barber station. Above his mirror and below a row of bright lights is a decorative license plate that reads "My Mama Says I'm Special"—a reference to *Forrest Gump*. To the left of the mirror is a large rectangular wooden decorative sign, the top of which reads: "Our Family Rules." Before "Rules," Chico wrote in "Chico's Cuts." It now reads: "Our Family Chico's Cuts Rules." The rules are as follows: "Share. Be kind. Love one another. Say please and thank you. Keep your promises. Be silly. Do your best. Say I'm sorry. Smile. Be patient. Don't whine. Hug one another often." Just outside the restroom is a counter where Chico keeps a small microwave and a near daily cup of espresso. On a shelf are Minion figurines. Chico is a fan of the yellow, pill-shaped creatures who speak nonsense. Every detail makes it Chico's Cuts. But there was a time when its future seemed uncertain. In May 2015, a few months after he'd first opened the shop, Chico was here one night—cleaning the AC unit. It was sometime after 8 p.m. When Chico was done, he got on his red motorcycle and rode out, heading westbound toward Forty-Ninth Street. He says he was just cruising. At that time, nearby, another man had backed his pickup truck onto Thirtieth Avenue North and into another car that was stopped in the turn lane at the intersection. When the truck driver fled the scene, he slammed into the rear of Chico's motorcycle. "He struck me from behind," the barber recalls. "So he hit me, pinched me under his truck."

News reports of the incident said the truck driver never made an attempt to avoid Chico. The barbero was dragged more than a hundred feet, and his motorcycle another ten blocks. Witnesses chased the truck driver down until police arrived at the scene. He was arrested and charged with DUI causing serious bodily injury and a slew of other charges.

Chico spent a month in a hospital with life-threatening injuries. For two weeks, he was in a coma. He still has a photo of himself in the hospital saved on his cell phone. In it, Chico is lying on a hospital bed. He is intubated, his eyes closed. His forehead is scraped and bloodied. So is his nose. He has a neck brace on. Monitors are on his chest, recording his vital signs. Chico remembers several doctors tending to his multiple injuries. One focused on his brain, and the other two focused on his collarbones, back, and other bones broken as a result of the crash. Several weeks later, Chico was discharged from the hospital. By September, he was back at work.

Chico can still recall a conversation he had with one of the doctors—a cubano like him—during a follow-up:

He asked me, "Where you from?"

"I'm Cuban."

He said, "How you got here?"

And I said, "Well, I came here when I was fifteen years old. I came in a raft. It was five of us in a raft."

So he said, "You came in a raft. You made it. And now this happened to you, and you made it? Man, you blessed, 'cause you went through all that, and then you made it now. You're still alive."

And I'm still here at the shop. After all that stuff that I've been through in life, I'm still here.

He said, "You blessed, man."

Not only did Chico come back. He came back stronger.

There are four barber chairs, but Chico's is the only one that is filled. He's a one-man shop at the moment. Like any business, he says, people come and go. Everybody's got a different mentality. Chico tells me there are barbers who start in a shop and think they're going to make a lot of money right away. It doesn't work that way. "A lot of barbers, they're not patient. They just come and go, and then they jump around and jump around. And then you can never make it because, every time you jump around, you lose clientele. People are not gonna follow you. Some people are gonna follow you, but not everybody. So anytime you jump, you gotta start from scratch." There are times when all chairs in the shop are filled. This happens. Some barbers move away, and others—as he says—come and go.

So how does Chico feel, seeing the other chairs emptied? Chairs that could bring his business more money? "The good thing, I'm not stressed," he says confidently. "That's the main thing. I'm not stressing for the money because I knew I could make it by myself. When I opened, I opened by myself. I can make it by myself." Sure, it would be even better if he had barbers working here. Extra money helps with the bills. "I just got to think, *Stay strong and positive, and then it'll be better days.* You know, that's the way it works." Sure, Chico is hiring, but he contends it's hard to recruit and retain barbers. A lot of people come in, newly arrived from different countries, searching for work. But they don't yet have a Florida barber's license. "You gotta have a license to be legit," Chico insists. "See, I won't let anybody work at the shop without a license. Because, at the end of the day, I can get in trouble myself. So you don't want that."

If you want a job at Chico's Cuts, the requirements are as follows: You have to be kind. Chico prefers that you not bring problems or negative energy into the space. You don't have to be the sharpest barber, because you'll learn a great deal while on the job. Chico can help with your skills. "So even though I'm by myself, and I'm not making that money from the chairs, it feels kind of good because it's me and the client, one on one." The clientele here is diverse. Chico says just because he's Latino doesn't mean his work attracts only Latino clients. He's been cutting hair since 1996. At that time, there weren't many Latinos in this area of St. Pete. Chico recalls only knowing two Cuban families back then. Over the years, his clientele has grown to where he now has Black clients, European clients, Asian clients. "They come to me because of my work. And when your work is nice, people look for that."

Word of mouth helps. Chico offers an example of someone seeing one of his freshly cut clients in a store, or at work:

They be like, "Hey, who cut your hair? It's sharp, man."

"Oh man, he's my barber, man. Chico, man. You gotta call him."

That's how it works.

Once the job is complete, Chico uses a blower to remove excess hair clippings from his client's head. He then removes the cape from around Mark's neck. His longtime client gets up from the chair, pays, then walks over to the small counter where Chico has a cup of espresso with even smaller plastic cups. The Boricua car salesman takes one small cup and serves himself a shot.

When Mark walked in this morning, he didn't need to tell Chico what style he wanted. "Nah, he knows me already." And Chico didn't need to ask. "Once you got the regulars, I remember everything," the seasoned barber says. "I know each person, what they get. Unless one day he changes his mind and wants to change his style . . . But they don't got to tell me nothing." Mark estimates that this haircut will last him about two or three weeks. People at work compliment him on not just his hair but how his whole look comes together. He takes a sip of coffee. Before leaving, he has one more story he wants to share about Chico.

"I came in here and I told him, *Hey, Alex, it's my birthday.* So he takes care of me and everything like that. And then I go, *Hey, Alex, how much I owe you?* He goes, *Nah, it's your birthday gift.* Those are the things you put in a balance, and you got to realize that this guy has a good aura, that this guy displays good intentions, good motives. This guy has it. The whole package. And he will talk to you, and he'll become your psychiatrist."

Mark eventually leaves, and Chico is back to being in his small shop alone, waiting for his next client. He admits he never thought about having a big barbershop. The bigger the shop, the more overhead you have. Mo' money, mo' problems. Nor does he have aspirations to open a second or third Chico's Cuts someday. He enjoys staying in one shop. Low-key but still hustling. "I love what I do, I'm good at it, and then I enjoy cutting hair. To me, I get up every morning, and I'm happy to come here."

DAY OFF

Liset enters the bodega with a shopping list stripped down to the bare necessities. On this Wednesday morning in early February, she slips into the aisle of cooking oils and Spanish olives. There, on the bottom shelf, she selects a large bottle of naranja agria—sour orange marinade. She then makes a beeline to the back of the bodega for a seventeen-ounce bag of Ariel laundry detergent powder and a bottle of Clorox all-purpose household cleaner. Because Liset used to work here, she moves around with ease. She greets her former boss and catches up with a few of her old coworkers. And as she pays for the items at the register, Liset loudly teases that she isn't paid attention to anymore. She leaves the bodega, makes a sharp right, and goes next door to the coin laundromat.

It is Liset's day off from her new job, but there is plenty to do. "I'm resting from work," she chuckles, "but I'm working!" After leaving her job at Orlando Latin Market, Liset began working afternoons and nights at a McDonald's. She later left Mickey D's and now works at a company that washes and delivers clean linens to hospitals in Florida.

The laundromat is bright and airy this morning. Fans whir above as Liset walks toward the back of the business. She inserts a twenty-dollar bill into the change machine. Out come eighty quarters. Not all will be for washing and drying. It helps to have coins around for when she wants to buy a drink or snack. From home Liset brought two clear bags filled with dirty laundry. She opens them and unloads her family's clothes into three Dexter machines. She feeds #7, #8, and #10 with coins and the detergent powder. "I always buy detergent from the bodeguita. Muy buena," she tells me. "Because my daughter dirties her clothes a lot at the daycare. Sometimes the clothes end up looking like they should just be thrown away."

Liset wears a coral PUMA T-shirt and gray jeans. Her long hair is pulled back in a ponytail, and she wears small gold hoop earrings. She is in a good mood today. Life for Liset has improved steadily from when she first migrated here in 2022 from Cuba. "Those of us who arrive here usually struggle a bit at first," says Liset, who is from Cienfuegos, on the southern coast of the island. "Pero mira, I drive now!" Her light brown eyes glitter with delight. She never dreamed of driving in Cuba. It's very difficult to have a car there, she explains, and it's still uncommon to see women driving. "It's very rare. Men are the ones who usually drive."

The drums carrying her family's clothes begin to spin. Inside, sweaters and pants churn. Each door is a window into a storm of white foam. Alone in the laundromat, Liset takes a moment to reflect on her new chapter in the US. She has a message for other immigrants. "Don't despair," she says. Her voice is assuring. "Little by little, things will start to flow. Things will fall into place." She says they may feel down in the beginning and find themselves unable to achieve all the dreams they arrived with. "But little by little, life will start to reward you with those things. You'll begin to meet those goals—your dreams." Liset's own dreams are entrenched in her daughter. "For me, I really want to see her grow up with the opportunities I didn't have," she says wistfully. "I don't expect her to be better, but that she becomes who she wants to become. That she has the opportunity to do what she wants." In Cuba, for example, Liset says you can study what you like, but you can't always apply it to an actual career. The opportunities in her native country aren't ample like here in the United States. "If she wants to be a housewife, then she can be a housewife," Liset says. "But if she wants to be a pilot, for example, then she can be a pilot. Because she can achieve that here. Eso es mi sueño." That is her dream.

For now, Liset will have to stay at the laundromat a while. The clothes need to be washed and dried and folded. Afterward, she has to shop for groceries for the following week. Liset also needs to gas up her car, to not waste time doing so before a workday. And then there's the never-ending labor at home. "I need to clean the house," she says. The bulk of Liset's errands on her day off are for her family. But she hopes to do at least one thing for herself, and that is to recolor her hair. Liset's ponytail reaches down to her jeans' back pockets. Her hair is thin and wispy at the ends. "I had red hair before. And I bought a box dye thinking it was the color of rojo vino (red wine). And look at the color it took on," she says, pointing to her brown hair with a reddish tint. "Now I have to redo the red. When I dyed my hair over, it must have blended the dyes, so now there's no concrete color." She laughs sheepishly. "I'm like an arcoíris." A rainbow. Liset prefers to dye her own hair because she says it's more comfortable. She doesn't need to adjust her schedule to go to a salon, where she'll be stuck for hours. She has since bought another box of hair dye. This time, she is determined to achieve a brighter red. More vibrant. More vivacious.

And since it's Liset's day off, she'll find the time to try again.

A RIDE WITH MERCEDES

On the first day in October, Mercedes nearly forgets about an appointment she has with the Social Security Administration. She had received a letter from the agency in the mail, something she needed to sort out, so she had planned to go to the St. Pete office this morning. But a call came in from Cuba, and the appointment slipped from her mind. Instead, she sat on her couch early this morning, chatting with her family back on the island.

I don't know anything about this when I stop by Orlando Latin Market before work. Mercedes's daughter, Liuba—one of the cashiers—asks me if the office building is on the way to my job. I tell her I believe it is. She then asks me for a favor.

Could you please drop off my mother, Mercedes, at the office?

Of course, I agree to help. And that's how I end up escorting Mercedes. The older woman walks from their apartment nearby to the bodega, dressed in a long-sleeved black dress with small white polka dots and pink-beige slingback sandals. Her hair is short, gray at the roots, and from her earlobes hang small gold hoops. Immediately, I can tell she is a character. Mercedes talks a mile a minute and uses her whole body to communicate. She thanks me for the ride and won't stop talking. I already know I'm going to adore this woman.

We get in the car and soon are at the intersection of US 19 and Thirtieth Avenue North, waiting for the green light to make a right onto US 19. The directions to the office are on my phone, and I listen as Mercedes tells me about her call from Cuba. She explains to me how she almost missed her appointment because she was distracted this morning. Her family had finally received the package she sent them, very early. But there were items meant for different people, so they needed help knowing what was for whom. Mercedes asked that some of the items go to one of her daughters, and a few others to her niece. The rest has to go to her sister, who knew where the remaining items were destined to go. *I sent over coffee, toothpaste, soap, deodorant, seasonings—cumin, complete seasoning. I sent . . . It's this way?*

I point to the directions on my phone and assure her we will arrive in eight minutes. I ask Mercedes if we have to go on I-275. My app says so, but I want to confirm with her. *Ah, tranquila, tranquila,* she says. She tells me not to worry. *Don't rush. Let others rush. You go with calma, because God has timing for everyone.*

I nod, amused, and tell her we'll arrive in seven minutes now.

So . . . She restarts her engine. *I forgot what I was saying.*

I chuckle and remind her that she was telling me about how she had sent a package to Cuba, and had forgotten about her appointment. *Oh, yes!* She remembers now. *Just now, when I had seasoned the chicharos with saintly calm, and after I had taken my medication, because this morning I woke up with high blood sugar. So I sat down and said, "Well, I'm going to wait." When Liuba left for work, I said, "Well, let me get up and get the day started." Oh! I said hello to a neighbor who is also from Cuba. She greets me every morning. I told her, "Buenos días Mayra. How did you get up this morning? We are fine, gracias a Dios. Because just waking up, alive, opening your eyes and breathing is a great gift from God."*

La mujer no me deja hablar. The woman won't let me get a word in. But I am loving every second of her morning replay. Chatty people are my favorite kind of people. She then tells me about her aches. *Many aches,* Mercedes stresses, *pero bueno, we're keeping on. There's nothing you can't endure. I woke up with a pain in my jaw. The pain has subsided bit by bit. I feel the same aches and pains as always, the same ones I brought from Cuba. Because in Cuba I didn't leave behind any aches. They all came with me. Even though I didn't look back.*

I ask her to clarify. What kind of aches is she referring to? Did she mean body aches?

Sí, los dolores del cuerpo. And my right knee. I haven't been able to do a knee replacement because my insurance doesn't cover it. Imagínate. I have to endure that. I want to switch over to another clinic where there are Cuban doctors. I can see them and can communicate better.

I check on our ETA. I don't know where this story is going, but by now I am deeply invested. Two minutes left until we arrive at the SSA building. Mercedes continues her story. *They sent me a letter that said they couldn't pay my benefits this month because they were missing information. I received the letter on the 11th. And that same day, I called and called and called. And all those who were available were in English. I couldn't talk. So that morning I began calling again and again and spoke with three representatives. I called one and wasn't satisfied. I called another. This was the whole day. I spoke with the last representative and told her, "Mira, I'm a señora. I'm older. I'm ill. I can't go out in these streets, running around like a loca. I forget things. Understand?" So they gave me this appointment. They told me it was for the first of October, at nine in the morning. And I said, "OK, no problem. Give it to me."*

We finally arrive at the building. The parking lot is almost full. I find a spot and ease my car into it. Mercedes continues talking. *So I told her, "How can I help my daughter with rent, utilities, everything?" I am here because I'm here. Never in life have I ever missed an appointment.* I offer to see Mercedes inside. She picks a ticket—D932—and finds a seat. That's when the real waiting begins.

I want the world to know that I am very grateful to God, she tells me. Mercedes wants me to include this in her story. *Because He had promised me that He would bring me to the United States, to wait and to believe in Him. And I said, "Dios, if that's what you want, then that's what it'll be."*

THE BITCH FROM CUBA

Later that day, on my lunch break, I visit Mercedes and Liuba at their apartment. That's when I meet Kima. The nearly five-year-old dog belongs to Liuba's daughter, who is not home. Like the women in her life, Kima is from Cuba. She had arrived in the United States a year ago, alone, having traveled by vehicle with other dogs through Mexico. The small dog journeyed for five days.

Back in Cuba, Kima was doted on. And she's treated the same here in the States. On this Tuesday she wears a pale pink sweater with leopard print, and a beaded necklace that reads "GOOD GIRL."

Mercedes and Kima are inseparable. They stayed behind in Cuba when Liuba had left the country a few years ago. With Liuba gone, Kima got depressed. They had to take her to the vet. The depression returned when, the following year, Liuba's daughter Thalia migrated, too. "My mamá would carry her and rock her in the mecedora like she was a child," Liuba says. When her mother decided to come to the United States, Liuba recalls her saying she wouldn't come here without Kima. "My mother later said, *You have to send her there. Because if not, I can't go. And I won't leave her behind.*"

Liuba says, thank God, they were able to bring Kima to the US. They paid a service that transports pets. "I told them not to give her any food that could kill her on the journey," Mercedes recalls. "Because she's not used to eating any kind of food. The only thing she ate was chicken. In Cuba I remember the last chicken I bought her. It cost me 9,500 pesos, because she had to eat her chicken."

Mercedes goes to a room and comes back with a new outfit for Kima. She picks up the dog and places her on a cushioned gray chair. She lifts up Kima's hind legs and begins to unclasp the leopard-print outfit. "Mira la niña de 'ela. La niñita de 'ela," Mercedes coos in a baby voice as she strips the dog. The new outfit, a dress with a bright red tutu, falls on the floor. Mercedes picks it up and slips it gently over Kima's head. The dog doesn't make a sound. She lets her great-grandmother dress

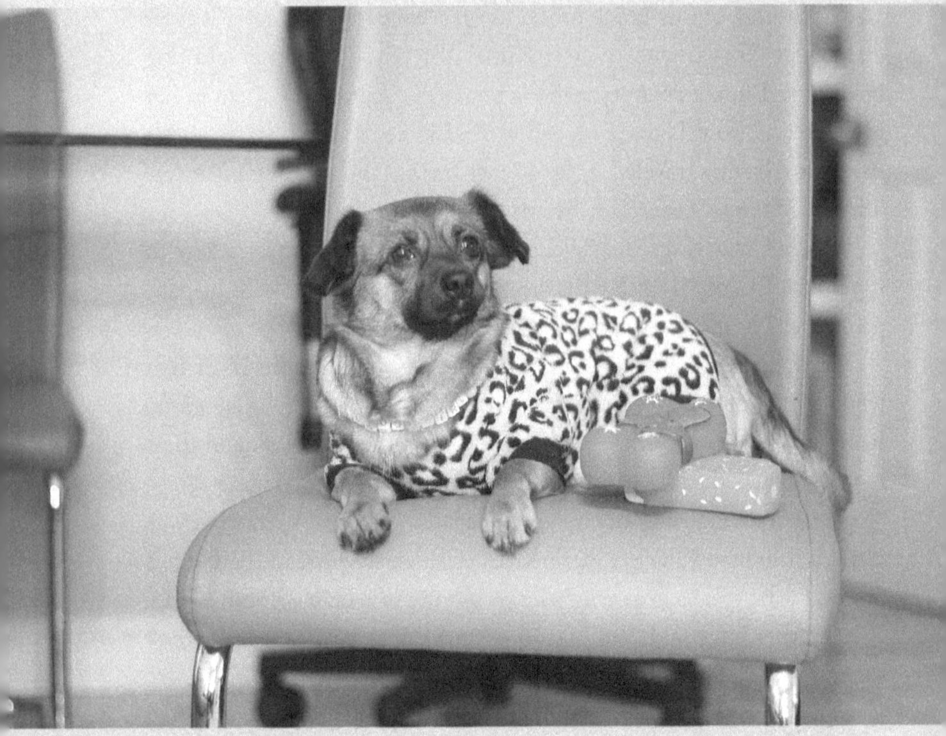

KIMA THE DOG FROM CUBA
IN HER NEW HOME IN
ST. PETERSBURG, FLORIDA.

her like the doll that she is. "We're going to make you bonita," she tells Kima. "And we're going out." The whole scene is endearing and funny, and I laugh with Liuba and Mercedes.

With the dress fully on, Mercedes ruffles the tutu with her hands and orders Kima to sit. Or stand. "Whatever is convenient for you," she tells the small dog in Spanish.

In many ways, Kima is the baby of the house. Liuba says Kima is very affectionate.

"And she's a señorita," she says of the dog, her tone serious. "She's never had a perrito."

FELO THE BODEGA CAT

We had a cat once. This was back when we lived in Brooklyn, in apartment 2B. Papi just arrived one day from work with this living, breathing animal that was unlike the rest of us. I can't remember how old I was exactly, but if I had to guess, I was maybe seven or eight. I thought, *Wow, my parents finally got us a pet.* His name was Felo, and he was adorable—small, black like coal, and quick. I fell in love. My brother and I shared a room, and the cat loved to hide under our armoire tucked in the corner. Felo would also hide under our wicker couch in la sala. And when he wasn't hiding, we followed him around, in awe of his every movement and leap. My brother desperately wanted to play with him, too, but Felo was shy. Or maybe he was afraid.

When I ask Mami if she remembers him, she brings up a rabbit. *It wasn't a rabbit,* I tell her. Though now I vaguely remember us having a rabbit at some point. *A gatito,* she confirms then. *What happened with the gatito?* Perhaps I am asking too much of my mom, to try to remember a blip of our life in Brooklyn decades ago. But I am not the type to let things go, and she knows this. *You don't remember that he brought this cat home, and I fell in love with it?* I ask her. I try to jog her memory and tell her how I thought we had finally gotten a pet. *Then one day,* I point out, *the cat was gone.* Mami guesses again: *It got lost.*

I correct her. *No, it didn't get lost, Mami. It was a bodega cat.*

Turns out Felo was not meant for us. *That cat was from the bodega,* Papi tells me. *I had adopted it for the bodega because there were some nuisance mice there. But then one day an inspector came by and said the cat couldn't be there. So I took the cat home for a few days until things cooled off.* Until things cooled off. That's what this was. Meanwhile, I'm here falling for a damn cat on some best-friends-forever-type shit. A bodega cat typically lives at a bodega and has one important job: to help control vermin like rats and mice. In recent years, the bodega cat has been catapulted into a beloved, unofficial mascot of New York City. It is an icon. There are social media accounts dedicated to bodega cats. Books have been

FREDDY WITH A BODEGA CAT
IN BROOKLYN, NEW YORK.

written about bodega cats. There are even T-shirts with bodega cats sitting pretty on the counter, curled up in coffee cups, or lounging on bread loaves. But I want to excavate this memory. I want to understand. So I ask my father if the city didn't allow bodega cats in the nineties. *No,* he tells me. *They said no, there couldn't be animals in the bodega.* But even if that were true, bodega cats were everywhere. Papi saw them all the time in other stores, including those that belonged to his friends. *And I told the inspector, "You're telling me there can't be animals. But mice are animals."* We laugh. Papi has always been quick with the jokes. He says the inspector laughed at that, too.

I ask my father if he ever thought about how bringing a cat home would make Fredito and I think that this was our pet. I don't remember him explaining any of it to us. *No,* he says plainly. *I didn't think about that. The only thing I thought about was hiding him from the inspector.* He chuckles. I tell him I fell in love with Felo. And then one day, he was gone. I want Pa to dig deeper into this memory with me. But he just laughs, sounding amused. *Así es,* he says. *That's how it is.* I tell Mami that I would have loved to have more pets as a child. She asserts that our apartment was too small for one. I counter that she doesn't like animals anyway. Then she proceeds to tell me she does like animals, but not to have them in the house. OK, then.

Pa says the city inspector eventually came back to the bodega. And when the man didn't see the cat anywhere in the store, he left and never returned. That's when Pa brought Felo back to the bodega. And we were back to being a pet-less family.

I ask Pa what ended up happening with the bodega cat. *Felo got sick. I don't know if it was something he ate. I took him to the veterinarian. They gave him some medicine.* Felo later got sick again and died. I tell Pa I am really sorry to hear. *Was he a good bodega cat?* I want to know.

Oh, yeah, Pa answers. *Whenever he would catch a mouse, he would bring it to me so I could see it.* That makes me laugh. I picture Felo, the cat that was never ours, presenting his prize. *He'd do that,* Pa tells me, *to show that he was doing his job.*

A CONVERSATION WITH TÍA MARGARITA

Standing at the end of the aisle of sweets with Tía Margarita while she prices desserts.

AMARIS: Tía, before this job, had you ever been a bodeguera before?

TÍA MARGARITA: I had never worked in bodegas, no. [Adds prices to merchandise with a price gun] But nothing is impossible en la vida. You have to learn a bit of everything in life. When I worked in factories in Nueba Yol, I didn't know how to do things. They would ask me, *Do you know how to do this?* And I'd say, *Bueno, I don't know—but I can learn.* And I learned. Porque uno no nace sabiendo. You are not born knowing. So I would learn.

AMARIS: How did you end up working here?

TÍA MARGARITA: Part-time, out of the need for money. I worked on Sundays at first. I worked at a daycare from Monday through Friday. On Saturdays I would wash clothes, clean the apartment, and all that. And on Sundays, I'd come here to work. That's how it began. I needed extra money.

AMARIS: When you first started working at the bodega, how did it go for you? What was your impression of the job?

TÍA MARGARITA: Bien. I was delighted because I talked to everyone. It didn't compare to how we have to work now. [Laughs] Now it's five or six times the work from back then. Before I would spend time talking with customers from different countries—

AMARIS: So you used to talk more than you worked?

TÍA MARGARITA: And now we work more than we talk.

[Laughter]

TÍA MARGARITA: We work hard here.

AMARIS: Yes, but it's also good. You like to talk.

TÍA MARGARITA: Yes, I talk, but it's not the same. Before, I would talk to people, get to know them more. Pero ahora es fuerte. It's intense now. It's a lot of work. I leave work on Saturdays and Sundays . . . because here it's not just physical. It's mental, too. It's: *Búcame eto'* [*Get this for me*]. *Where is this? Why does this item have this price, and not that price? Get me this. Where is this thing? Are you going to order that?* All day. You leave work mentally tired.

AMARIS: In the end you're like, as Dominicans say: *Yo 'toy explota.* [*I'm depleted.*]

TÍA MARGARITA: [Chuckles] Not so much. But it's enough. Saturdays and Sundays, for me, are difficult now. With the time I have left in life, I want to go out, hang out with a friend, drink a coffee, go to the store even if I don't buy anything.

AMARIS: Tía, but why do you say with the years you have left?

TÍA MARGARITA: Bueno, because I don't know how many I have left. If I have ten or twenty years. I can see me reaching up to ninety or so, but I don't know if I will make that.

[Both chuckle]

TÍA MARGARITA: I can see myself at ninety-four years old, still putting on lipstick.

AMARIS: Ay, que linda.

A CALL TO PAPI ON THE EVE OF HURRICANE HELENE

PAPI: Espérate. Déjame peinarme, déjame peinarme.

AMARIS: Let you brush your hair? But this is a phone call.

PAPI: Anda, sí. Tell me.

AMARIS: [Laughs] Papi, oye. How are you?

PAPI: We're fine.

AMARIS: That's good, Pa. I wanted to ask. There's a hurricane headed our way tonight. What are you going to do tomorrow with work? Are you opening the bodega?

PAPI: We're going to open if it's not too bad. Because if it's really bad, if there's a lot of wind and a lot of rain, we don't think we'll open.

AMARIS: Ah, okay, okay.

PAPI: Depends on how it is in the morning.

AMARIS: Ah, okay. Because the store is in St. Petersburg, and you don't live there.

PAPI: Yes, and we have to also take care of the employees. When there are hurricanes that are imminent, that they're for sure heading here, we don't open.

AMARIS: Ah, okay. Well, in this case, here comes one.

PAPI: Sí, but it's not the same category as the others.

AMARIS: Who decides who will open or not? You or Mami?

PAPI: Tu mamá es la jefa.

[Both laugh]

AMARIS: You always say that, but you're also the boss.

PAPI: No, she's the boss. Ella es la mayimba.

AMARIS: La mayimba. That's true.

MILTON

A different energy pulsates through Orlando Latin Market. People are worried, concerned, anxious. It is Sunday, October 6, 2024. Florida is under threat. Inside the store is a frenetic symphony of sounds. The beeps of the register. The crinkling of plastic bags being stuffed with groceries. The endless airing of everyone's preparation plans. The low murmur of customers talking to themselves about what they still need. Some will hunker down at home, or take what they can with them for evacuation. The governor of Florida has declared a state of emergency for more than thirty counties, including all in the Tampa Bay area. Hurricane Helene just devastated the state's Big Bend region, and now another one is coming. Tropical Storm Milton is expected to become a dangerous hurricane, one that could hit the west coast of Florida. It's expected to bring with it winds that damage and storm surges that can endanger lives.

Shortly after 2 p.m., Papi asks Mami to lower the music playing on YouTube, probably so he can hear himself think. So down in volume goes "No Hay Cama Pa' Tanta Gente" by El Gran Combo de Puerto Rico. My father, dressed in a bright sea blue T-shirt and long dark gray joggers, stands before the green wooden shelves. One by one, he nestles one small bag of red beans after another, until there's a small, neat pile in a cardboard box on a shelf. The food display in the front kitchen is almost cleared out. Chicharrones, crispy and savory, have flown out of there. So has the congrí, Cuban black beans and rice. A man standing by an endcap fills his blue basket with Cuban crackers. A woman runs her hands through a pile of batatas, examining each sweet potato before slipping them into a clear bag. Another woman, dressed in a lavender-blue shirt and shorts, picks up two bright yellow bags of Charras corn tostadas. A young man trails behind her, with a stack of flour tortillas in his arms. My Tía Margarita comes from around the corner near the front kitchen and zooms past me, her hands filled with plátanos. "Mira," she tells me. "One's for me. One's for you." A man in a long-sleeved navy-blue sweater pushes a cart filled with cases of water.

Tropical Storm Milton will soon make landfall. And we'll continue to prepare, then brace ourselves.

LA OFICINA

(STORAGE ROOM)

previous THE INSIDE OF LA OFICINA, A MULTIPURPOSE STORAGE ROOM AND BREAK ROOM AT ORLANDO LATIN MARKET.

A PIECE OF CUBA WITH ME

On an unusually cold January morning, Deisy sits in the room we call la oficina in the very back corner of the bodega. This room is multipurpose. It is like an almacén, a warehouse, with shelves of Styrofoam containers for hot food, stacks of soda cans in cardboard carrier trays, and boxes stacked high of canned guandules. It's also where a few workers go during their break, to eat their lunch. And it's where you can find some privacy for conversations. Deisy is surrounded by stacks of Styrofoam containers on wooden shelves and boxes filled with fruit nectars. Her dark hair is pulled back in a ponytail, and she wears leggings and a black sweater with a daisy screen-printed on it. A former cashier at the bodega, Deisy still visits often to catch up with her old coworkers by the register and front kitchen. She'll grab something small to eat for breakfast and sip her coffee before work.

Beneath her sweater, a map of Cuba can be found on Deisy's skin. The tattoo, like the island country, is broken into fifteen provinces. "That's the map of my island," she says. "I see it everywhere—in geography, in schools, in everything." All are shaded gray except for one that's a rosy pink. The standout is Cienfuegos, where Deisy was born. Behind the inked map is the country's flag—known as la Estrella Solitaria. Its bright blue stripes are made to look like waves where the Caribbean Sea, Gulf of Mexico, and Atlantic Ocean meet. The ripples of turquoise and Pacific blue appear to run underneath the body of Cuba. The flag's cherry chevron begins on Deisy's upper to mid-back. The red ink outlines what should be a white five-pointed star. But in this tattoo, her skin fills in the gaps. Deisy paid an artist in Cienfuegos 1,250 Cuban pesos for this constant reminder of their country. The design took about three hours. "I knew I wanted something that had to do with my country. Tú sabe? That had to do with my homeland, with my idiosyncrasies, with mi isla, with mi tierra. And that was the map."

Around the time Deisy got the tattoo, she had been trying to leave the country. Twice, she says she tried to obtain a visa to go to Spain but was unsuccessful. She and her boyfriend then obtained a visa to Mexico and crossed the border, fulfilling her desire to leave Cuba in 2019.

When asked why she chose the tattoo of Cuba, Deisy shifts her hips slightly on her seat, a case of Coca-Cola bottles wrapped in thick plastic. "Because, eh . . ." A heavy sigh takes the place of her voice. "For me, it's like I brought a piece of Cuba with me," she says. "It's what I brought from my country. Because I'm not going back to Cuba." Deisy's voice splinters in pain. She quickly draws her hands up to her face, fans it to keep tears away. She has no desire to return to Cuba. She has no family left there. She says she doesn't want to go back until the current government is eliminated. "The Cuban government is a failed state," Deisy says plainly. "If the government is unable to maintain the nourishment, the education, the health of its people—the basic needs—then you're useless." But that's communism, she adds matter-of-factly. Deisy likens communists to owners of their respective countries, who keep the people in la ultima miseria. In ultimate misery, extreme poverty.

Since the 1959 Cuban Revolution—the Fidel Castro–led armed uprising that forced dictator Fulgencio Batista from the island nation—many Cubans have left. Their migration to the United States has occurred in waves. There was a brain drain, with doctors and dentists choosing to leave. A large number of businesspeople also left. Many primarily ended up in Miami. In 1965, Castro, unhappy with the negative press the island received over Cubans risking their lives at sea to make it to Florida, announced that those who wished to leave the island could do so. Cuban exiles who wanted to pick up their loved ones would be permitted to sail to the port of Camarioca, located on the island's northern coast. This boatlift made way for the Freedom Flights, an airlift of twice-daily flights between Cuba and Miami that ran through 1973.

The Cuban Adjustment Act of 1966 allowed Cuban natives to apply for permanent residency after just one year, which essentially fast-tracked them to attain citizenship and voting rights. More than a decade later, over several months in 1980, another mass emigration of Cubans arrived from the island's port of Mariel. The Mariel boatlift, as it was called, saw an estimated 125,000 Cubans (nicknamed Marielitos) cross

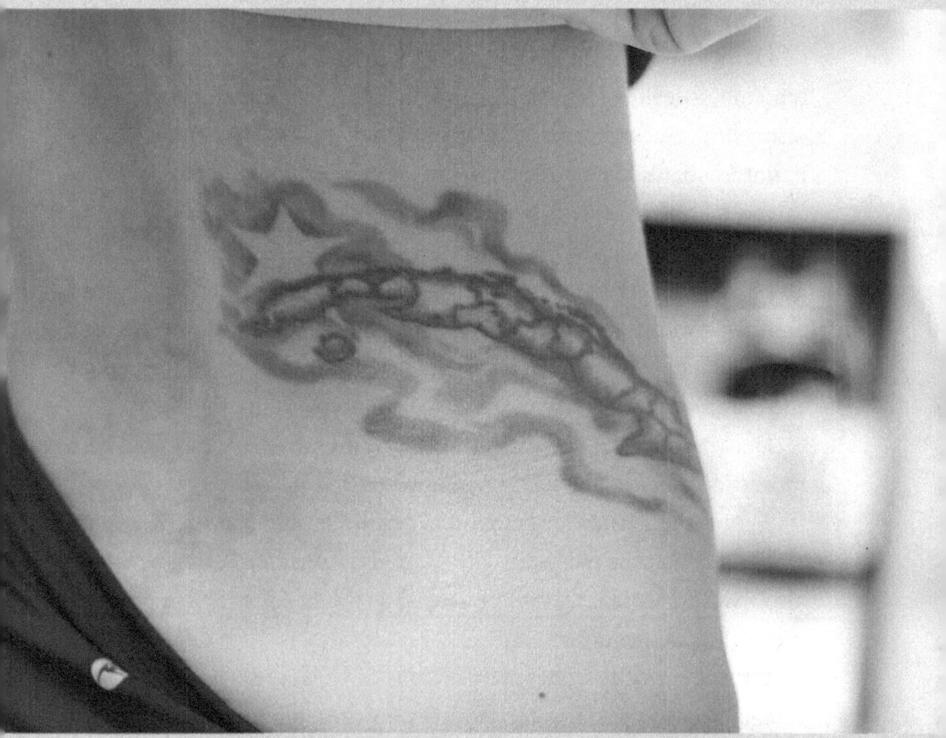

DEISY SHOWS HER TATTOO
OF THE MAP OF CUBA,
WITH THE FLAG AS RIPPLES
OF THE OCEAN.

the Straits of Florida to the US. Then, in the 1990s, more Cubans left during the Special Period. The island saw yet another huge wave of migration during the crisis in 2021, in response to economic hardships and other uncertainties.

Deisy arrived in the US in 2019 and, in 2024, became a citizen. She remembers feeling like she was born again. "I will live here for the rest of my life." But even though Deisy's in the United States now, she remains a cubana. Cien por ciento, she says. One hundred percent. "Now I'm both." She chuckles. "Now I'm happy speaking Spanglish. Now I'm cubana and americana."

By now Deisy has more tattoos. A silhouette of her family, and another inspired by Antoine de Saint-Exupéry's *The Little Prince.* But the Cuba tattoo, inked while still there, represents how she feels about the island she was born in. About the country's reality.

Deisy admits she no longer thinks about Cuba every day. Life here moves too quickly. She works and now has a family of her own to tend to. When the island does cross her mind, Deisy reports feeling only sadness. When she meets up with her old friends from Cuba who now also live in Florida, they reminisce about their school days on their island. Happy memories.

But the majority of her recollections of Cuba are of misery. Of the hunger she says she and her family went through. Of the scarcity. Of the frequent power outages. "When you talk to people there, they tell you there's no electricity, there's no water," she says. "And that's what breaks my heart. It makes me very sad. It makes me sad because we live so good here. We have everything. By working you can cover all your necessities. And to know that there are so many people—eleven million people—living in a jail, that they don't have the possibility to have anything. They live in la miseria."

Beyond sadness about the state of Cuba, something else tugs at Deisy. "Es como añoranza," she explains. Like a yearning. "I really miss my malecón."

Before Deisy and her husband welcomed their daughter, they brainstormed names. Like her tattoo, Deisy knew she wanted a name that had something to do with their native country. She didn't like the name Cuba. She thought of Habana, the capital. "But I'm not habanera," Deisy points out. And she laughs when she admits that Cienfuegos, where she was born, would not be a suitable name for a niña. Their daughter was born in 2021 in St. Pete, and Deisy and her husband finally settled on the one. The Spanish word for *island.* They named her Isla.

MUCHO TRABAJO Y MUCHA SALUD

Damaris sits on a step stool ladder in the office/storage room. Her body leans against one of two chest freezers that run the length of a wall. Behind her are tall shelves filled with Styrofoam containers for later use by the front kitchen workers. Today my mother wears an apron over a light blue T-shirt and pants, and her hair is pulled back. Her left elbow rests on the freezer, and she lays her head on her left hand. It is shortly before 11 a.m. on New Year's Eve, and the bodega vibrates with customers and workers. She is tired.

I ask Mami to describe this past year. "Muy bien," she tells me. Very good. She rubs her left eye. "This year has been, gracias a Dios, filled with good health and a lot of work." She nods her head, deep in reflection on this past year. "Mucho trabajo y mucha salud," she repeats. Her mind appears to be elsewhere. "Gracias a Dios," she says again—this time quieter than before. Her hope for the new year is that God gives her and everyone in her life continued good health. "Y trabajo como siempre," she said. And work, like always. Work is how you pay bills, your mortgage. How you pay to rest on vacation.

"To the Dominican Republic?" I ask her.

"Well, wherever," my mother responds. "As long as I leave here. Maybe we'll go to Colombia." I ask her if she slept well the night before. I then pull a Mami move and tell her something she's always telling me.

"Tú te ve' cansada." I tell her she looks tired. Damaris rakes her hair with her fingers.

"Ah, it's just that this is every day," she informs me. "And I can't leave your father alone, you know. But today we close at four. I'll leave and I'll lay in my bed." She lifts her head, drawing out the last few words. As if she only needs to blink to teleport home.

Looking ahead to the new year, Damaris hopes for continued good health for her family. And that they stay united. She also vows, like many women, to take better care of herself. "Take better care of my health, eat better, walk. People always say that, but they never do it," she says. "But this year, I'm going to be more conscious of what I eat. I'm going to try to take better care of myself."

ANA THE SANTERA

The volume is raised a bit when Ana walks into Orlando Latin Market. She talks loudly and play argues with Freddy and Damaris in her signature Cuban sass. Whenever Ana stops by the bodega, she stays for a while. She sips café from a chair behind the register, as if she actually works here. Here, she feels at home. Ana is a longtime customer, a close friend of my parents, and one of their vendors. Years ago, she operated a boutique right next door that was later turned into Chico's Cuts.

On this Saturday in April, Ana strolls into the bodega in a white dress. She greets the workers one by one. Her tight curls are wrapped under a white turban, and her feet don a pair of fresh, white Pumas. Ana la cubana is the embodiment of modern ritual and has been for some time. Nearly a year ago she began her initiation into Santería. I want to know more, so Ana joins me in la oficina. I bring her a chair so she can sit, and we talk. An Afro-diasporic religion formed in Cuba, Santería has its roots in the traditions of the Yoruba people from present-day Nigeria and Benin who were enslaved and brought to the island. Once in Cuba, Spanish colonizers tried to force Catholicism on the enslaved. In order to protect and maintain their religious traditions, the Yoruba began practicing in secret. In time, Santería—also known as Regla de Ocha—developed as a syncretic religion that blended both Yoruba and Catholic traditions. There is no key sacred text that unifies its practitioners. Rather, beliefs have been handed down orally through generations and are typically practiced in people's homes. What devotees of Santería are seeking has been generally described as a good life and to live in harmony with themselves and the world around them.

Ana says her family back in Cuba practiced Catholicism but didn't believe in Santería. The Catholic Church does not officially recognize Santería, and some Catholics shun the faith. Others are hostile toward it. Still, Ana insists that parallels can be drawn between both religions. Practitioners of Santería worship and make offerings to deities known as orishas—sometimes syncretized with Catholic saints. "My saint is

Changó," Ana says. Changó, sometimes spelled Shango, is considered a powerful orisha closely associated with thunder, lightning, and fire. "In the Catholic Church," Ana points out, "it's Santa Bárbara." Saint Barbara is a popular saint venerated by Catholics as the patron saint of artillerymen and miners. She is also considered a protector against sudden, violent death, lightning, and fire. "Ochún, in our religion, is la Caridad del Cobre [Our Lady of Charity]," Ana continues. With ease she rattles off more names of saints and spirits: Oyá and Yemayá—the latter most closely associated with water. Ana points again to syncretism, the practice of combining different beliefs.

Ana la cubana is an iyabó, the term often used for initiates into the faith. Iyabós follow a complex initiation process. For an entire year, they typically dress in white, from head to toe. Their heads must be covered. The white is said to represent, among other symbols, peace of mind. The mother of three says her health—specifically a bone disease—compelled her to begin the initiation process. "I got better thanks to the religion," she shares. "I feel really good. Spiritually, I'm at peace." During the initiation process, iyabós experience certain limitations and prohibitions in behaviors, food, dress, and other aspects of daily life. Ana is prohibited from eating guayaba or eggs. And she has to stay away from clubs and alcohol. "These are things you have to do, if you want everything to work out in the end," she says.

At the time of our interview, Ana is not permitted to be photographed. Not in the storage room or in the bodega. Nowhere. She is a vision in white, with a few meaningful pops of color on her person. On her right wrist are nine brown bangles, and on her left are three bracelets—two made of different colored beads, and a single silver bracelet. A long necklace of polygonal white and red beads hangs over her dress.

After the 1959 Cuban Revolution, Santería, like Catholicism and other religions, faced official persecution by Cuba's communist government. Religion was suppressed for decades after. In the early 1990s, Cuba relaxed religious restrictions, declaring the country a "secular state" rather than an atheist one. Religious life on the island continues to grow and diversify. Santería has also grown in its visibility and popularity.

Ana maintains her religion has given her better health. Santería has taught her so much. One year and one week of wearing all white and refraining from certain things will not mark a specific milestone for her. It is merely a necessary step toward an existence of better health and peace. She tells me this is for life.

TWO YEARS AND THREE MONTHS

Alcides enters the bodega one morning for some frituras—chicharrones and croquetas. A few things to savor, plus something to wash it all down. We are about two weeks into the New Year, and the customers who come in, Alcides included, arrive bundled in coats and beanie hats. Freddy greets his longtime customer. And, like a spark, a years-old memory resurfaces between the men. It happens often when Alcides stops by Orlando Latin Market. This particular story is etched in the minds of both the camagüeyano and the store owner. Because the bodega is bustling this morning, I lead Alcides to la oficina in the back of the store where it's quieter. I want to hear this story. There are no chairs in the room, so we stand in the space between stacks of boxes and the chest freezers. A hoarse laugh erupts from Alcides as he shares the story. One day, years ago, he entered the market with his dog, Coco—a white poodle named after Alcides's favorite fruit.

"Yo andaba bebido," admits Alcides. He was drunk that day.

"And I told him, *Alcides, tu no puede' entrar aquí con ese perro,*" my father recalls later. The store owner told Alcides he couldn't enter with his dog. Pets weren't allowed inside, he explained to his longtime customer.

"Y entonces yo le dijé, *Vámono', Coco. Que aquí no no' quieren,*" Alcides recounts. *Let's go, Coco. We're not wanted here,* the man announced to his dog, slurring his words. Turned on his heels and left.

A bunch of people witnessed the comical moment.

Alcides tells me he figured he was allowed to bring his dog into the bodega that day. Here, he sees dogs at malls. Everywhere you look, there are dogs. Which is why he didn't think twice before walking in with his own in tow. "And because I was used to going into different places with him, and they didn't let me bring him here, and I was drunk, I said, *Bueno, vámono', Coco. Aquí no no' quieren.*"

The construction worker returned to the store the next day as if nothing had happened.

Coco is no longer with Alcides. The beloved poodle died a few years back. After Coco's death, Alcides says he helped raise Tito, a pitbull that belonged to a friend. Then Tito went into cardiac arrest and died. There will be no more pets for Alcides. "I've had many pets in this country," he says. "And every time something happens to one, it affects me. And I decided not to have any more."

No more pets, and no more alcohol for Alcides. He is sober now. "It's been two years and three months since I stopped drinking. And I'm proud of that. I'm not drinking ever again," he says. "I drank for forty-five years and it caused a lot of damage to me, to my family, to my well-being, to my finances. It damaged everything. And I decided to never drink again."

Alcides has had many problems in this country, including two DUIs and an accident. He says he spent twelve years without driving. "I turned in my driver's license myself. I went to the police and turned in my license when I didn't want to drive anymore."

He admits to still drinking when Coco was in his life. He'd drink every day. Alcides points to his family tree. There were other alcoholics in his family, he notes. Habitual drinkers. "I'm sober now," he says. "And I want to stay that way."

MAMI'S MANGÚ

I stop by the bodega on my lunch break. It's late January. I have lost count of how many times I have visited Orlando Latin Market this year. For months I have observed my mother, perpetually tired and on her feet, working. My father, too. I have dropped into the bodega before work, during my lunch break, for a few hours on select Saturdays or Sundays. I want to observe the inner workings of the store, to interview any person willing to share a piece of their story with me. I want to know how Mami's doing on any given workday.

We exchange kisses. And immediately, she picks up a plátano and begins peeling. It is technically time for me to eat something. It's my break. I am hungry. If I am truly honest with Ma, I would tell her I care more about seeing who I could talk to for this project than about eating. The food can always wait. But I know my mother. Admitting that would launch her into a lecture about how I don't take care of myself. I had made a conscious, perhaps wild decision to juggle a full-time job, my blessed children, and book projects. All of those factors probably led to her frequently force-feeding me unsolicited consejos (advice): *You're going to have your bodega book and your other librito. No te metes en mas cosas. Don't get into anything else. You have to make time for yourself. And for your health. Ya tú sabe. Not even if they offer you $60,000. Nada. Your peace is more valuable than that.* She always thinks I am inventando, which is Dominican for doing the most. Deep inside this rant is a mother's love. I know this because I am a mother myself now.

For a good part of my adulthood, I have felt this bit of tension. My mother's maternal instincts go off when she thinks I am taking on too much. And perhaps I am. But this is how I am wired. I have this one life, and I want to fill it till it bursts at the seams. Call it self-actualization. But as I've gotten older, I have grown to understand my mother's love languages. They are acts of service, quality time, and worrying about the people she loves most. And I love her for that. When I was a third grader at P.S. 316, I wrote a Valentine's Day message for Mami. I found it in an old photo album in my parents' house. The message was typed in all caps, in Courier New. The white sheet of paper was cut into a heart shape.

> DEAR MOM I LOVE YOU WITH ALL THE PIECES OF MY HEART. I REMEMBERED WHEN I WAS SICK AND YOU TOOK GOOD CARE OF ME. I HOPE YOU LIKE THE LETTER BECAUSE I TOOK A LONG TIME TO FINISH THIS LETTER. WELL ANYWAY I LOVE YOU VERY MUCH AND I HOPE YOU NEVER DIE BECAUSE I LOVE YOU WITH ALL MY HEART. MOM, MAYBE I COULD BUY YOU A PRESENT, IF I GOT ENOUGH MONEY TO BUY SOMETHING FOR YOU. I GOT A POEM FOR YOU, HERE IT IS; ROSES ARE RED, VIOLETS ARE BLUE, SUGAR IS SWEET AND SO ARE YOU. I LOVE YOU SO MUCH.
>
> YOUR DAUGHTER,
> AMARIS

Mami cuts the green plantains long, then drops them in a big pot of water on the industrial stove in the back kitchen. *I always tell your papá, because when he's busy with his boat, he sometimes forgets to eat or anything—I tell him, "Bueno, if you don't have your health, you don't have your boat." That's the same thing I tell you. If you don't take care of yourself, you won't have a book.* She has a point. My dad is obsessed with fishing, obsessed with his boat. Maybe I take after him. With the fire on high, it doesn't take long for the water to boil. Mami grabs a large stainless-steel spoon and dips it into the pot to stir the plátanos. The spoon's bowl goes underwater, dipping the plátanos this way and that, around and around. The long wedges are buoys in dark waters. A brewing storm with rising steam. "Is that going to be ready by the time I have to leave?" I ask my mom.

"Yes. You just arrived," she scolds me. "And you said you would be here an hour."

I look back at the green plantains. It's tricky for me to tell with my naked eye when they are all completely soft. The only true test is to poke a piece of plátano with a fork or knife. If the chunk is still hard, then it needs more time. If the fork pierces straight through the flesh, you're good. And it doesn't matter if I need to stab it several times to make sure. These boiled plátanos are destined to become mangú, anyway. Mashed.

A minute later, we are together in the front kitchen while Mami washes a pan.

"You're going to return to work smelling like chicharrón," she cautions me.

Though she is warning me, there is warmth in her tone.

"It's okay," I tell her. There are worse smells.

She brings the pan over to the back kitchen and places it on the front burner.

"Te ayudo?" I ask her, offering to help but knowing I'm just in her way.

She shakes her head no as she presides over the pot of boiling green plantains. My mother's brown hands are beautiful and worn from work. Swiftly and effortlessly, they move the pan to another burner and add cooking oil to it. Her right hand turns the second burner on. The oil soon begins to heat up. Her hands cut a chunk of queso de freir into small squares and fries them in the pan.

Less than ten minutes later, once the plátanos have softened to Mami's liking, she drains the pot of its water. She smashes the green plantains. Plucks the fried cheese chunks out of the second pan. Then she gets a plate bordered with decorative palm trees and fills it with mangú and a handful of pieces of cheese. With a knife, she cuts an aguacate into geometric shapes. Places those on the plate, too.

My mother then hands me the food of her labor and cautions me not to get my work clothes dirty.

Steam rises from the meal. I bring it to the storage room in the corner of the bodega. Mami brings me a chair to sit on before stepping out again. I rest the plate on one of the chest freezers because there's no table in this room. The mangú is soft in my mouth, savory. I count five pieces of cheese, half of which are brown and crispy. My first bite into one emits a crunch sound. Delicious.

DAMARIS AND HER BABY DAUGHTER,
AMARIS, RELAXING IN RÍO NIZAO
IN THE DOMINICAN REPUBLIC.

A short time later, she returns to check on me.

"Gracias, Mami," I say. "You made those with what?"

"With what?" she asks.

"With love?"

"Sí," she replies. "I make everything with love."

BULLETIN BOARD IN SEPTEMBER

Nails, Uñas

Like always, the bulletin board itself is filled with mostly ads for efficiency apartments or houses for sale or rent. One ad reads in black marker and all caps: "EFFICIENCY DISPONIBLE." In the lower left corner, someone is renting out a "mobi home" with everything included. Another ad for an efficiency for rent stipulates that it's only for one person: "1 persona sola." There is also a house for sale in a fifty-five-plus community, newly remodeled with two bedrooms, one bath. Fully furnished. Those interested can only send a text to a number with a 407 area code. On the flyer are four photos of the home, but the images are obscured from view by someone else who placed their own ad for a room for rent on top.

Do you want long-lasting, beautiful nails? You need not look further than a tear-off flyer on the brick exterior outside Orlando Latin Market's bulletin board, a few feet away from the other flyers and advertisements. On a white sheet are promises of a job well done: "Calidad. Quality. Creatividad. Creativity. Detalle. Detail. Modernas. Modern. Duraderas. Durable. Manos. Hands. Pies. Feet. Cubana. Cubana. Cubana." Does that mean the technicians are all cubanas? Maybe. You can find out for sure if you call the number listed on one of the pastel tabs at the bottom. Area code is 727. Below the flyer is an ad for a Catholic school, with scholarships available. Two brown girls in burgundy uniform shirts smile at the camera. The ad beckons you to "APPLY TODAY."

One business card in a pretty font is hanging vertically by a white pushpin. If you crane your neck to the left, you can read the small print. A jewelry repairman, at your service. Below it, more ads for efficiency apartments. One pale yellow flyer states that there's an efficiency for rent with parking spots for two cars. It's apparently located in one of the best areas of St. Petersburg. Call and ask for Julio.

Just outside the bulletin board, to the right, is a black-and-white flyer for a family festival during "el mes de la Hispanidad." A celebration for Hispanic Heritage Month with food, music, dance, community resources, and more. Below that is a bilingual flyer from a small insurance company. A bullet list has its offerings: "Obamacare. Seguro de auto. Car insurance. Seguro de casa. Home insurance. Work compensation. General liability."

TÍA MARGARITA'S LAST DAY

I meet my dad outside the bodega and hand him the red roses and cake I bought on behalf of Mami, who isn't working today. They're for my Tía Margarita. It is early November. Today is my aunt's last day of work at Orlando Latin Market. Ma wanted to make her older sister feel special.

11:20 a.m.—Papi walks toward the entrance. He clutches the bouquet of roses sprinkled with baby's breath in his right hand. Holds the cake in his left hand, like a restaurant server does a tray. The door whistles as it opens.

Tía Margarita is walking by and, on seeing Papi, stops.

"Ahhhh!" She screams in surprise and breaks into a cackle.

"Feliz retiro," Papi tells her.

A kiss on the cheek.

"Ayyyy, gracias," Margarita says.

Her fuchsia-colored lips stretch in delight. She is beaming.

I bring her balloons. Another kiss on the cheek.

"Gracias. Ooooh," my aunt says.

She receives the roses and cake from Papi.

A customer at the register remarks on the scene unfolding.

"She's the boss, but she's retiring," Liuba, the cashier, tells the man. "She doesn't want to work anymore."

Tía Margarita erupts in laughter.

"Hoy es su último día!" I inform him and anyone else who can hear. I follow my aunt, who heads straight to the front kitchen.

"Look what they brought me," she announces to the other women.

She proudly holds up the bouquet in her right hand, the cake in her left.

"Tirame una foto ahí," Margarita orders. She wants me to snap a photo of her.

"Look, here, with them," my aunt adds. She goes to stand next to Nayví.

"Okay, wait," I say, laughing.

"Come, Lisandra," my aunt tells her other coworker.

The two women in their plastic aprons pose next to my aunt.

"Oh, I love this cake," Margarita says, tilting it for a closer look.

The three women look up at me, with smiles.

Still laughing, I stop the video to snap a photo.

11:23 a.m.—Minutes after the impromptu photo session, Tía Margarita stands in front of the carnicería. She tidies the plastic containers of manteca—pork lard—on the deli counter. Behind the manteca is one of her balloons. It sways gently.

"Where did you tie it?" I ask her. "By the lard?"

"Sí," she says. "There."

She lifts her arm toward the balloon and continues working.

Someone congratulates her on her retirement.

"Gracias, gracias!" Margarita replies.

11:24 a.m.—Back bent slightly forward, Tía Margarita places a bunch of cilantro into the hollow metal container, where the fresh produce can be found.

"Lindo," she says, mostly to herself.

She adjusts a bunch of culantro, too, as if they're a bouquet. She then turns to me.

"Here we are, on this last day," she says.

Margarita says this with elegance, posing again by the bunches of cilantro and culantro.

"On the last day that I'm going to be at the bodega," she tells me.

She throws her head back and claps once.

I ask her, "And how do you feel?"

She picks up another bunch of culantro and combs through the serrated leaves with her right thumb.

"I feel good," my tía says. She laughs again. Turns around and looks at the cashier, then back at the produce.

"Me siento bien," Margarita says again. "Another chapter in my life realized. Now I'll rest more, take it easier. Try to go out more with my friends."

"So what you're saying is that you're tired of the bodega?" I ask jokingly.

"No, no, no!" she laughs. "It's just that now I can relax more and I can try to go out more with friends."

This is a cycle, she tells me. My aunt makes a big circle with her right hand, still clutching the culantro bunch.

"Life is about cycles that you close," she says.

Both arms move in circles now.

"And this is one more cycle of my life."

She nods her head.

12:28 p.m.—Margarita walks into the bodega freezer. She picks up the cake we brought her, a Strawberry Elegance cake from Publix. I had seen the round mound of sweet, topped with chocolate ganache and glazed strawberries, and thought, *This is a fitting cake for my Tía Margarita.* It is dressed up, like she always is.

"I'm going to cut the bizcocho," she says aloud to her coworkers in the front kitchen. She places the cake on the counter where Cuban sandwiches are prepared. My aunt opens the disposable plastic container.

"Already?" asks Nayví.

"Yes," Margarita says.

Nayví thinks it's a bit early to cut a cake.

My aunt disagrees.

"No, because more people arrive later," Margarita says. "And you know we leave at four."

She lifts her head to see if there are any customers waiting to order food.

"It's only 12:30 p.m.," Nayví gently protests.

"But then more people will come," Margarita repeats.

She reaches above the display case for a stack of foam hinged-lid containers, to fill with slices of cake. Nayví approaches Margarita from behind, grabs onto her shoulders and then lifts her up playfully. Tía's laugh punctuates the air.

"Ayy, I'm leaving," Margarita says. "I'm going to be missed here, eh?"

Nayví lets go and nods her head.

"We're going to miss you," she tells Tía. "We're going to miss you."

"Awww," Margarita says. "Ay, gracias que me van a extrañar."

She pulls the first two containers from the stack and places them on the counter, next to the cake. With a knife, she pierces the chocolate ganache and cuts the first slice.

1:50 p.m.—Margarita stands behind the register counter. Liuba rings customers up, and my aunt bags their items. The bodega buzzes with customers.

"I want to dedicate more time to myself," my tía says.

She places her manicured hands over her chest and closes her eyes. She says she wants to meditate and relax more. Brings her hands up to the air, then brings them down slowly. Lifts her head up, then snaps back to reality.

She glances back at me and bursts into laughter again.

2:52 p.m.—In the back of the store between the glass bottles of mango nectar and the tall fridges containing beer, a collection of flattened cardboard boxes fills a shopping cart. The longest box, blue with the words JUMBO ROOTS (Product of Ecuador), is nearly Margarita's height. She spins the cart around so she can push the handle forward.

"I'm going to discard these cartones," she said. "Por última vez."

She laughs and turns right, straight to the store's entrance. Once outside, she goes left and down the ramp. The cart's wheels rattle against the gravel parking lot. She takes a cardboard box with hand holes. Lifts the black lid of the commercial dumpster and throws the box in.

Margarita grabs more flattened boxes, two or three at a time, and adds them to the pile.

3:37 p.m.—"Let me go put this in the car," she says.

From behind the register Margarita carries a few black plastic bags filled with different items she'd picked up from the store, plus her bouquet, and steps out.

"I'll be right back."

3:42 p.m.—Tía Margarita, back behind the register, stands before the shelves lined with body sprays and plucks a pair of dangling keys. She leaves the store again.

To her immediate left are five mismatched shopping carts lined up between the bodega's brick exterior and window, and a hoop barrier. Security chains hang from the steel bar.

Margarita bends forward and, with the key, opens the padlock holding the somewhat rusted chains together. She then unravels the chain and loops one end of it around the first cart. Threads the chain underneath the handles of the others, including the last. She's securing the shopping carts for the night so they're not stolen.

It's fifteen minutes until closing time.

"We have to turn off the 'OPEN' sign," Margarita says over the clink-clanking of the chain. "Store away the cabbage, the culantro, the cilantro. We have to put those away."

3:59 p.m.—"No te pierdas, Tía!"

Liuba, the cashier, is telling Margarita not to disappear now that she'll no longer be working here.

The key to lock the store is in my tía's right hand. She jumps in place, out of joy. One minute till closing.

"Adiós!" she tells her soon-to-be-former coworkers. "It was a pleasure for you all to know me."

We all laugh. Everyone files out of the store now. A purse is hooked onto my aunt's left arm and she brings with her a bottle of water.

"Ay, Jesus," my aunt murmurs. She closes the entrance door behind her. Kisses the metal frame. The coworkers look on, laughing at her elaborate goodbye. At her show. She turns to them with the key in her right hand, raises it so we can all bear witness. She then inserts the key into the lock and turns it clockwise.

"Por última vez," the carnicero tells my aunt with a smile. He is expecting her to hand him the key. One last time. "Espérate," she tells him. Wait. She turns the key again. Successfully locks the door. She turns to her coworkers again and dangles the key in front of her. Margarita purses her lips as if she's going to whistle. She then begins to drop it low and bursts into laughter again. Finally, she passes the key on.

The scene is very Cuban, very Dominican. The voices and loud laughs are a bittersweet nod to the end of Margarita's tenure here.

She stands up again.

"Okay!" she says.

She tells us all goodbye, struts down the length of the storefront down the ramp. Like a model on a runway. One final time as an employee.

STORIES ABOUND

My Tío Mingo—one of Mami's five brothers—partially blames the bitter Brooklyn winters for his eventual move to Florida. My parents, my brother, and I were already living here, among the first in our huge family to leave New York City for the Sunshine State. In conversations with my uncle back in NY, my parents told him about the climate, about the humidity and summers. Those phone calls gave Mingo the curiosity to, as he says, "aventurar." So he did. He embarked on a new adventure. My tío left his job in New York for the promise of Florida, with its humid subtropical climate in closer proximity to the Dominican Republic. He moved into my parents' house and slept in a bedroom carved out of the garage just for him. And he soon joined the family business. At Orlando Latin Market, Mingo stocked merchandise. He ensured there were always enough canned beans on the shelves, that they were lined up neatly. My tío made a ton of new friends, most of them Cubans. He helped some who had recently arrived in the US with paperwork and passport applications. He helped others obtain medical benefits.

It was also here that Tío Mingo received what he still thinks about years later: an education on Cuba and its history from the mouths of its people.

There are many stories from Cubans, and what they went through in Cuba with Fidel Castro's government. It went from a democratic country into a country that was not democratic, but a dictatorship. In Cuba, Castro isolated those who didn't support him or his ideas. He maintained power for many years. In Cuba there was a lot of hunger.

And there were many "brecheros" [*a kind of voyeur or someone who meddles into others' lives*]. *Let's say you're cubana or cubano. When you arrived at a barrio, they had a system in which they found out where you came from, why you moved away from your pueblo, if you were anti-government. I can't remember what the name was that they used for this, but the government used those people in the neighborhood to find out who it was that arrived there. I heard many stories like this at the bodega. Muchísimas historias. Some were against the Cuban government. Others weren't and worked for the government, to keep an eye on those who had moved to a particular area.*

I felt bad. I'm Dominican and I haven't had a government so anti-democratic like Fidel Castro's. I was a boy during the time of Rafael Trujillo. He died in 1961 and I was born in 1957, so I didn't know anything about the era of Trujillo. Later, when I was older, I learned a great deal about who Trujillo was. That he had a lot of compadres to get closer to their women. You understand? Un mujeriego.

I enjoyed working in the bodega very much. I worked with the products that would arrive. I would receive them and put them on shelves. Stock. For me it wasn't hard work. Almost all my friends there were Cuban. We would talk and hang out together on the weekends, especially Luis and Lazaro. We would visit each other. I heard many things, like how they arrived in the United States from Cuba. They told incredible stories. In Cuba, many of them had to move from one place to the next because they were being watched by the government. It was there that I came to know part of the reality of Cuba. I still think about those stories. They've stayed with me.

When I came here to the United States, I enrolled in Hostos Community College in the Bronx. There I took literature classes, and that's when I was shown the greatest writer of Latin America: Gabriel García Márquez. "Cien años de soledad," "El coronel no tiene quien le escriba." I said, "Wow, he has some imagination. It's incredible the imagination he has." He opened my mind. Que manera de contar lo que es incontable. What a way to describe what is indescribable. You understand? Because he hadn't lived through any of that. That was from his imagination. Literature is a world outside of the real world. I like stories based on true events. But I like stories from the 1900s. I was born in 1957, so that's to say I saw how the world was at that time. For example, I've always been a reader. We have a maestro de cuentos—Juan Bosch. I read him, too.

When I lived in St. Pete I would go to a library that's on Seventieth Avenue North. When they would have used books for sale, sometimes for a dollar, I would say, "Wow. This book interests me. And mira, for one dollar. I'm going to enjoy this dollar." And I'd go to the library in Brooklyn. I like to read. I don't write, but I always have something in here [my mind] to write at a later time. Even songs. I sometimes think, "Let me see if I can create a song."

It's the same thing that must be happening to you. Much of what you write, you haven't lived. But I think one of the greatest things is the mind of a human being. It can think, and it can write.

UN VERANO EN NUEVA YORK

This must have been sometime in the early eighties, if memories serve, because Mami said she was eighteen years old at the time. One summer day, she stopped by the Flatbush bodega where Papi worked. She couldn't find him inside. There was only one other place he'd be. The door to the store's underground was open. She looked through there, and there Pa was, in the basement surrounded by glinting glass. All around him were empty bottles. *And there he was, sweaty and organizing the glass bottles,* Ma recalls. *You had to put the ones from Coca-Cola with Coca-Cola, the Pepsi with Pepsi.* She stayed there a while. *I was like eighteen years old. I had to look at the belleza. Ya tú sabe—an eighteen-year-old in love. We were novios.*

It was scorching that day. The type of calor that makes you not wanna leave your house, period, let alone work. *With a calor, ya tú sabe, en un verano en Nueva York,* Ma remembers. With that New York summer heat.

But Pa was so focused on the task at hand that he hadn't looked up. Hadn't realized that someone was staring at him. *After a little while, I noticed that your mamá—Damaris—was sitting on the stairs, watching me.*

Mami's Tía Carmen lived in the area. So after watching her boyfriend work for some time, Damaris said goodbye to him and continued on to her aunt's house. *She was watching how I worked,* Pa recalls. *She was seeing that she was going to get a hardworking man.*

GRATITUDE

On the day before I have to submit my manuscript draft, I call up Papi. It's a Sunday in late March. He and Mami are at the bodega, working. Pa isn't near his phone, so one of the cashiers answers and passes it to Ma. I tell her I want to speak to her and Papi, together. "I'm almost done with the book," I tell them, "and I want to thank you both for letting me follow you and the bodega for a year."

"Okay," Ma says.

"Okay," Pa echoes. "De nada, mi amor."

"What else?" my mom asks in Spanish.

I wonder how they feel about the project.

To Mami, this project marks a chapter in their lives—the good and bad. Papi says he is very happy that I realized this dream of mine, and that other people took part so it could become a reality.

At this moment, emotions surge in me. A rising tide of love and deep gratitude for my parents. I am six again, at our old Brooklyn apartment, opening Christmas gifts not from Santa Claus but from them. I am back in the past, attending art classes at the Brooklyn Museum because my mom sees that I love to create with my hands. I am at the library, checking out piles of books with her and Fredito. I am a child, listening to boleros in Papi's Jeep as he drives us to our next adventure. I am fifteen, in Santiago, on the way to a quinceañera photo shoot arranged by Mami. Even though I didn't want a quince, she insists we should still mark this special year of my life. I am in my thirties, crying to my father on the phone after my family was in a horrible car accident. He drops everything to come be with us. Time and time again, they have answered my calls, supported me. I think about all the times I have felt on the verge of crying, all the times I just wanted to know what they were up to, all the times I just wanted to hear their voices.

"I wanted to say that I wouldn't be able to do this without you," I say, my voice breaking. "So thank you."

"You know we're always here for you, mi amor," Papi says sincerely.

I am crying now, but I manage another thank-you.

"Tomorrow we'll help you with the kids, so you can have your margarita!" my mom cheers.

I laugh through my tears. A margarita was the prize I swore I would have once I submitted this manuscript. I thank her. "I'm very proud of you both," I tell them. "Because through my reporting, people have told me really good things about you." I want them to know, I see them. I see their hearts. I am proud of them not just because they are my parents, but because they show love and goodwill to others. They are not perfect. No one is. I'm certainly not. But it is a wondrous thing, to set out to tell the story of a place and come away with feeling the many beating hearts inside it.

I mean it when I thank them for everything. Absolutely everything.

ACKNOWLEDGMENTS

This book—at its root and in every iteration—would not exist without my parents. Damaris and Freddy Castillo built Orlando Latin Market into a community anchor with their sweat, tears, and countless sacrifices. And in doing so, they taught me how to always push forward no matter how difficult life gets. Mami y Papi, gracias por todo el amor y apoyo incondicional que me han dado. Quiero que sepan que estoy muy orgullosa de ustedes dos. Han logrado tantos sueños con su propio sudor y tremendo sacrificio. Ma and Pa, thank you for not only loving me but for always supporting me in my dreams y locuras. Even when you didn't quite get the magnitude of this project, you agreed to let me do my thing. I hope you see this as our thing now. Thank you for giving me your blessing to take this on, and for allowing me to interview you again, and again, and again. Thank you for being wonderful parents and grandparents. You both are my biggest inspiration in life.

My deep gratitude goes to every person who spoke with me for this book. Stitching *Bodega Stories* together would not have been possible without your consent. You all chose to let me in, to grant me your precious time, and to share pieces of yourselves with me. I am sorry I could not fit in everyone's stories, but I am forever grateful for your time and generosity. It was an honor of a lifetime to get to know each and every one of you. I wish we could do this all over again.

Stephanye Hunter, you have been a great source of encouragement throughout this process. I could not have picked a more enthusiastic editor for *Bodega Stories.* Thank you for always responding to my emails, even the neurotic ones. We did it. A heartfelt thanks to Romi Gutierrez, Marthe Walters, Rachel Doll, Şevval Erçin, Mindy Basinger Hill, and the entire University Press of Florida team for your care and commitment to this project. Thank you, David Hazouri, for your whimsical illustrated map of the bodega. Thank you, Lori Rider, for your keen-eyed copyedits. It takes a village to raise a book, and I'm really happy to have raised my very first one with y'all. I am also grateful to the

University Press of Florida's editorial board. Thank you for the green light. Can't tell you all how anxiously I waited for it.

Erika Morillo and Annabelle Tometich, your careful readings as peer reviewers of this project were a gift. Thank you for your generous and thoughtful feedback, which were all in tremendous service of this book. I am forever honored you both said yes.

Thanks to the Authors Guild and to Alison M. Steele for all your help as I negotiated the terms of my book contract. Thanks, Craig Pittman, for your advice and for the recommendation. Thank you, Angie Cruz and Angy Abreu, for all your encouragement throughout my writing journey. Thanks to every author who shared their insight with me while I was still mulling this whole thing over.

Thank you, Stefanie Sanchez Von Borstel, for all your encouragement and support. You are a wonderful literary agent, and I am really happy that we get to work together.

Thanks to my brother, Freddy, for eagerly listening to snippets of stories as I wrote this book. Your enthusiasm kept me going. Love you, manito.

To my big, wonderful family for supporting me: Abuela Ula, Titi Rosi, Tío José Onésimo, Tía Margarita, Tío Julio, Tía Morena, Tío Mingo, Tía Yolanda, Tío Romeo, and all my tíos and tías—including those who have passed on but live on in our memories. I come from a family of natural-born storytellers, one of whom is my Tío Juan Báez Melo—a literary giant in DR and in my eyes. I cherish every visit to Librería La Trinitaria to see you. Love to Nadya, Aniell, Samuel, Esther, Evelyn, Nancy, Richard, Merfred, Maria, Lucio, Charo, Ivan, Ambar, Lyanne, Nixa, Alexandra, Osmar, and my many other cousins both in DR and in the States. Love to my bonus family: Sandra, Dominique, Nathalie, Jonathan, Mariano, Nubia, Mauricio, and Emily. Love to the Sierra and Cardona families. Thank you all for supporting me.

Thanks to the authors who took time to read this work early and write generous blurbs: Erika Morillo, Annabelle Tometich, Claire Jiménez, Amina Gautier, and Angie Cruz. You all understood what I was trying to do with this book, and that alone was more than I could ask for. Thank you, thank you, thank you.

Thanks to my wonderful mentors for sharing your publishing lessons and wisdom with me: Natalia Sylvester, Monica Brown, Arely Guzmán, and Yamile Saied Méndez.

I am so lucky to have friends and colleagues who have supported me through this process and who have listened to me ramble excitedly about this book when it was still in fragments. Your encouragement meant so much. *Takes deep breath.* Thank you to Tatiana Sánchez-Rivera, Angela Fu, Erika Brito, Emely Collazo, Ileana Najarro, Gloria Muñoz, Laura Vasey, Stefanie Crespo, Ashley Cisneros Mejia, Janive Santini, Ricardo De La Cruz, Rosa Rodriguez, Kori Tuitt, Kayla Randall, Emily Wood, Indhira Suero Acosta, Kelly McBride, Nicole Slaughter Graham, Ren LaForme, Janine Morales, TyLisa C. Johnson, Tom Jones, Ellen Hine, Andrew DeLong, Jessica De Leon, Lissette Norman, Dalys M. Gilling, Marilyn Flores, Karina N. González, Loreben Tuquero, Maria Briceño, Alanna Dvorak, Gabe Echazabal, Caryn Bush Baird, Salvador Rodriguez-Ruiz, Alondhra "Aloe" Suarez, Urpi Rodas Vásquez, Wally Rodríguez Bustinza, Ashley J. Collins, Ashley Lyn Espinoza, Maria Carrillo, and of course my book madrina Lane DeGregory.

Thanks to all the organizations and publications that have supported me along the way: Periplus Collective, Las Musas, Latinx in Publishing, *Kweli* Journal, We Need Diverse Books, the Brooklyn Caribbean Literary Festival, *Aster(ix)* Journal, the Dominican Studies Institute of the City University of New York, and the Dominican Writers Association. Shout-out to the talented writers I built community with through the Inlandia Institute. Please keep writing. I am also grateful to have met so many talented authors through the years. It is a joy to read your stories.

To the historians and scholars who work tirelessly to document our histories, thanks for the important work you do. We have so much to learn from you all. My respect to journalists for reporting the first, and sometimes the only, draft of history. My admiration to those who have worked in bodegas or continue to grind in them. I see you, and I hope you saw yourself represented in the pages of this book. A salute to all the storytellers and artists who care about bodegas and remind us why they're important.

Honorable mentions to Crown Heights, Woodhaven, libraries everywhere, bookworms everywhere, independent bookstores, merengue *and* bachata, therapy, and yoga. And thank you, coffee, for making me (falsely) believe I can do it all.

If I forgot anyone, please forgive me as my brain was mush by the time I wrote this. Truly. No one tells you how much pressure it is to write this damn page. But know that I really appreciate your support.

To my husband, Geo: Thank you for supporting my writer dreams and for all those times you held down the fort at home so I could spend much-needed time to write. This book would have been impossible to pull off without you. I love you.

To Camilo and Gianni: I hope one day you'll both read this book. And when you do, you'll see that, if your mother could do this, you can do anything. Do not be afraid to dream, even when what you want feels out of reach. I will always be there to encourage you and cheer you on. Mami loves you both with all my heart.

SOURCES

FROM QUISQUEYA TO NEW YORK CITY

Duany, Jorge. "Los Países: Transnational Migration from the Dominican Republic to the United States." In Ernesto Sagás and Sintia E. Molina, eds., *Dominican Migration: Transnational Perspectives.* University Press of Florida, 2004.

Hoffnung-Garskof, Jesse. *A Tale of Two Cities: Santo Domingo and New York After 1950.* Princeton University Press, 2007.

Mansel, Tim. "I Shot the Cruellest Dictator in the Americas." BBC, May 28, 2011. https://www.bbc.com/news/world-latin-america-13560512.

Sagás, Ernesto, and Sintia E. Molina. "Introduction." In Ernesto Sagás and Sintia E. Molina, eds., *Dominican Migration: Transnational Perspectives.* University Press of Florida, 2004.

BROOKLYN BODEGA BEGINNINGS

Claiborne, Craig. "Puerto Rican Food Market Flourishes Here; Public Shopping Site on Park Ave. Sells Unusual Products." *New York Times,* January 8, 1959. https://www.nytimes.com/1959/01/08/archives/puerto-rican-food-market-flourishing-here-public-shopping-site-on.html.

Hoffnung-Garskof, Jesse. *A Tale of Two Cities: Santo Domingo and New York After 1950.* Princeton University Press, 2007.

Sanabria, Carlos. *The Bodega: A Cornerstone of Puerto Rican Barrios (The Justo Martí Collection).* Centro Press, 2016.

Sánchez Korrol, Virginia E. *From Colonia to Community: The History of Puerto Ricans in New York City.* University of California Press, 1983.

Shanahan, Ed. "Grand Theft A.T.M.: A Bodega Crime Wave Hits New York." *New York Times,* July 2, 2025. https://www.nytimes.com/2025/07/02/nyregion/nyc-atm-thefts.html.

THE OG BODEGUERA

Hoffnung-Garskof, Jesse. *A Tale of Two Cities: Santo Domingo and New York After 1950.* Princeton University Press, 2007.

CAN THEY BE A WITNESS?

Martínez-Fernández, Luis. *Revolutionary Cuba: A History.* University Press of Florida, 2014.

JESUS IS HER ANSWER

Delerme, Simone. *Latino Orlando: Suburban Transformation and Racial Conflict.* University Press of Florida, 2020.

SOUP JOUMOU

Germain, Jacquelyne. "Haiti's Beloved Soup Joumou Serves Up 'Freedom in Every Bowl.'" *Smithsonian,* December 30, 2022. https://www.smithsonianmag.com/travel/haitis-beloved-soup-joumou-serves-up-freedom-in-every-bowl-180981378/.

Heroes: Principles of African Greatness. Smithsonian National Museum of African Art. https://africa.si.edu/exhibitions/heroes-principles-african-greatness.

Lindskoog, Carl. *Detain and Punish: Haitian Refugees and the Rise of the World's Largest Immigration Detention System.* University of Florida Press, 2018.

Mohl, Raymond A., and George E. Pozzetta. "Immigration and Ethnicity in Florida History." In Michael Gannon, ed., *The History of Florida.* University Press of Florida, 2013.

Scanlan, John, and Gilburt Loescher. "Human Rights, U.S. Foreign Policy, and Haitian Refugees." *Articles by Maurer Faculty,* Maurer School of Law, Indiana University, 1984. https://www.repository.law.indiana.edu/cgi/viewcontent.cgi?article=3495&context=facpub.

Vree, Matthew, and Alison Satake. "Haiti's History." Frontline/World Rough Cut, 2007. https://www.pbs.org/frontlineworld/rough/2007/12/haiti_belos_sonlinks.html.

BARRIO BOYS, BARRIO BROTHERS

Hoffnung-Garskof, Jesse. *A Tale of Two Cities: Santo Domingo and New York After 1950.* Princeton University Press, 2007.

EL CARNICERO

Frank, Marc. *Cuban Revelations: Behind the Scenes in Havana.* University Press of Florida, 2015.

Frank, Marc. "Cuba Loosens Ban on Cattle Slaughter, Sales of Beef, Dairy." Reuters, April 14, 2021. https://www.reuters.com/world/americas/cuba-loosens-regulations-killing-cows-selling-beef-2021-04-14/.

A SOMBRERO ALWAYS, SIN PENA

Ferrer, Ada. *Cuba: An American History.* Scribner, 2021.

Martínez-Fernández, Luis. *Revolutionary Cuba: A History.* University Press of Florida, 2014.

A PIECE OF CUBA WITH ME

Duany, Jorge. "Cuban Migration: A Postrevolution Exodus Ebbs and Flows." Migration Policy Institute, July 6, 2017. https://www.migrationpolicy.org/article/cuban-migration-postrevolution-exodus-ebbs-and-flows.

Triay, Victor Andres. *The Mariel Boatlift: A Cuban-American Journey.* University of Florida Press, 2019.

ANA THE SANTERA

Acevedo, Claudia. *Orishas: Cuban Syncretism and Spirituality.* Aurelia Ediciones, 2018.

Palmer, Colin A., ed. *Encyclopedia of African-American Culture and History: The Black Experience in the Americas.* 2nd ed. Thomson Gale, 2006.

ILLUSTRATION CREDITS

Page ii	Photo by Amaris Castillo
Page x	Courtesy of artist David Hazouri
Page 7	Courtesy of the Castillo family
Page 14	Courtesy of the Castillo family
Page 25	Photo by Amaris Castillo
Page 37	Photo by Amaris Castillo
Page 44	Photo by Amaris Castillo
Page 56	Courtesy of the Castillo family
Page 60	Courtesy of the Castillo family
Page 65	Courtesy of the Castillo family
Page 68	Photo by Amaris Castillo
Page 71	Photo by Amaris Castillo
Page 73	Photo by Amaris Castillo
Page 90	Photo by Amaris Castillo
Page 104	Photo by Amaris Castillo
Page 114	Courtesy of the Castillo family
Page 118	Courtesy of the Castillo family
Page 123	Photo by Amaris Castillo
Page 131	Photo by Amaris Castillo
Page 135	Photo by Amaris Castillo
Page 146	Photo by Amaris Castillo
Page 159	Photo by Amaris Castillo
Page 162	Photo by Amaris Castillo
Page 170	Photo by Amaris Castillo
Page 186	Photo by Amaris Castillo
Page 190	Courtesy of the Castillo family
Page 197	Photo by Amaris Castillo
Page 201	Photo by Amaris Castillo
Page 214	Courtesy of the Castillo family

AMARIS CASTILLO is a Brooklyn native and daughter of Dominican immigrants. A former newspaper reporter, her work has appeared in the *New York Times*, the *Lowell Sun*, the *Bradenton Herald*, and elsewhere. She received a BA from the University of South Florida and an MS from Columbia Journalism School. She currently works at the Poynter Institute for Media Studies and lives in the Tampa Bay area with her family.

www.ingramcontent.com/pod-product-compliance
Lightning Source LLC
LaVergne TN
LVHW092134170926
848365LV00033B/619